DAMEON GIBBS

The World Around Them

Commentaries of An Early 20th Century School Teacher

GIBBS PUBLISHING
CONGLOMERATE

First published by Gibbs Publishing Conglomerate 2025

Copyright © 2025 by Dameon Gibbs

First edition

ISBN: 978-1-966856-04-7

Translation by Jason Illari
Translation by Dameon Gibbs
Advisor: Jason Illari

This book was professionally typeset on Reedsy.
Find out more at reedsy.com

Contents

Preface

The following pages have been coined *Humphreys' Commentaries* by the transcribers. Judging by the penmanship and the type of paper used, it appears the *Commentaries* were penned sometime during the first half of the 20th century, but pinpointing an exact date has proved difficult. Written by Miss Mary Elizabeth Humphreys of Salisbury, born September 25, 1881, daughter of Dr. Eugene and Josephine Tarr Humphreys, the essays explore early childhood education, a somewhat burgeoning science in the U.S. during the turn of the 20th century. Humphreys, a native of Wicomico County, writes about the theories and practices propounded by German pedagogue Friedrich Froebel.

Born in 1782, Froebel was the principle developer of the concept of Kindergarten, the Froebelian Method and *Froebel Gifts*. He advanced the model of free learning through play and taught that the senses needed to be engaged in children to inspire true learning. Froebel also believed that his lessons would aid children to use and visualize the natural world as a stepping stone to learning. Readers interested in the methods of Piaget, Harrison and Montessori should find *Humphreys' Commentaries* an interesting read as well.

Humphreys agrees with Froebel, and she underscores the positive impacts of his methodology throughout her work and quotes him extensively. She addresses directly some of Froebel's popular teachings which were often expressed through games and songs or objects called gifts. Wherever possible, we have footnoted Humphreys' sources to help readers identify historical references. Occasional spelling or grammatical mistakes made by Humphreys have been corrected in italics to ease readability but we have not attempted to change wording or sentence structure to be true to the quasi stream of consciousness tone of the essays.

Known as Miss "Betty" later in life, Humphreys is often remembered for her connection to the iconic Humphreys canon, "the General", now located in downtown Salisbury. The canon belonged to her grandfather and was donated to the city via the Wicomico County Historical Society in 1973, two years before her death on September 26, 1975. Her passion for early childhood education is somewhat of a mystery, but sources continue to be found which shed light on her school activities as a young woman. In the 1907 *Salisbury Directory* she is found living at home on Broad Street.She and her sister, Nellie, are both listed as "school teachers" in the directory.

A document published by the Bureau of Education in 1914 inventories all schools throughout the United States, and "Miss Elizabeth Humphreys Kindergarten" in "Salisbury, Maryland" is noted. It is one of only six Kindergartens listed in Maryland. Whether or not Humphreys taught in the family home on Broad Street or at another location is still to be determined. Humphreys' teacher accreditation diploma is speculated to have survived over the years, and remains in private hands in Salisbury. Further research will hopefully bring to light the diploma's exact date, and it was reportedly issued by a school in Baltimore. The *Commentaries* are graded- most are marked very good or excellent- and several contain special notations within the margins in someone else's hand, presumably Humphreys' teacher.

No teacher's name is ever identified, but we have included these comments within brackets to distinguish them from Humphreys' own text. We cannot say with any certainty that the papers are connected to the school in Baltimore or any other school in particular. Researchers wishing to delve further into the specific date and purpose of the *Commentaries* may wish to start their investigation by tracking down the Baltimore diploma and then investigate whatever records still exist from the Baltimore Kindergarten Association, the Maryland State Normal School and Maryland State Teachers College.

It should be underscored that the *Commentaries* do offer a substantial amount of content related to history, art, philosophy, ethics, and religion. References such as the following are riddled throughout Humphreys' work; "the life of all life, the light of all light, the love of all love, the good of all good-God" and "there are two things necessary to every life and that is first to discriminate the permanent and essential points in life from the accidental and vanishing elements."

After working on this project for several years, we are pleased to present the following transcription to help historians further understand the life of Elizabeth Humphreys, and explore the enlightening and sometimes mysterious subject matter contained in her manuscript. Readers can now more easily take a glimpse into the mind of an educator reflecting on childhood development at a time when progressive theories about the subject were gaining momentum in academic circles. The transcription will also help researchers interested in the history of education on the Eastern Shore and in Maryland in general.

The original *Humphreys' Commentaries* manuscript now resides at the Nabb Research Center for Delmarva History and Culture at Salisbury University, Salisbury, Maryland. Selected research materials have been included within the appendix. We are grateful to the Nabb Research Center, the Newtown Association, Webb-Burnett Law LLC, and to our numerous proof-readers who helped us complete this project.

-Jason Illari and Dameon Gibbs 2012

Note: Transcribers wanted to honor Elizabeth Humphreys' writings by keeping her writing structure, sentences, and paragraphs as originally written.

Acknowledgments

The transcribers would like to thank our many family members and friends who encouraged us over the years to persevere and complete this project. Special thanks goes out to our numerous proof-readers as well. Without their help, it would have been difficult to complete this project. Finally, we would like to acknowledge the Nabb Research Center's staff for their insightful contributions and support. We would also like to give another special thanks to *Dokia Design I* for their help in formatting this book.

Humphreys' Commentaries

By

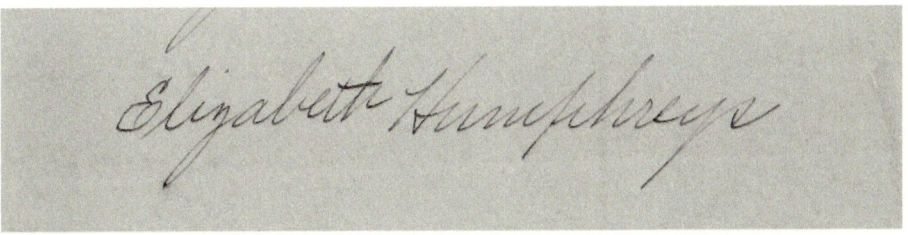

Collated, Transcribed and Edited: by Jason Illari and Dameon Gibbs

Games and Songs

Beckon to the Chicken and Beckon to the Pigeons

There is a universal need of sympathy in the human life. This is manifested in the child's love for animals. The child looks upon animals and knows that he has found comrades.Children see in "the looking glass of nature"[1] the energy which is in themselves. Life recognizes life. Whatever children feel in their own hearts they seek in the actions of their comrades. Beckoning the chickens sounds the call of life to life. Beckoning the pigeons is the answer of life to life.

One reason why the child loves animals is because they can respond to him. The real life of animals is symbolic. "It presents analogies to human emotions, relationships, and experiences."[2]

If sympathy is a universal need there is a universal answer. The Creator responds to universal needs. There is a direct response to our need of sympathy through nature.

The sense of sympathy or being one with all life is stronger in the child than the sense of distance. A child will reach out after the moon or other distant objects as though they were near by. This shows his feeling of oneness.

The life around the child as he sees it is a reflection of his own life. We see ourselves in nature. The outer life is a reflection, and through seeing this life outside of himself the child sees more clearly his own life. In order to see ourselves we must have the reflection of this outside life. It is well to give the

---

[1] Possible reference from *Froebel Gifts* or writing of William Blake, 1757-1827, English poet

[2] Possible reference from *Froebel Gifts*

child object lessons in nature especially with animals as the bond of sympathy is so strong between them. In this way he feels the stirrings of his own life. Unless the child is taught to see the lessons of nature he cannot understand it enough to see himself reflected in it.

"And since you know you cannot see yourself. So well as by reflection, I, your glass, Will modestly discover to yourself That of yourself which you yet know not."[3]

The basis of the power to see ourselves reflected in nature is the fact that we and nature come from the same source. There is sympathy between us simply from our relationship.

If the mother is a conscious one she will teach her child lessons in nature. This will be her safest way of opening the gates of life to him.

The ideal mother in the picture has her child in her arms. He is watching the turkeys and chickens. With delight he listens to their gobbling and *clicking*. Through his mother's efforts the child is seeing the life outside of himself and will feel his own life more keenly. In Froebel's own words "Each child has a vision of his own inmost life in the mirror of nature."[4] This inmost life gains fresh strength through beholding its reflection.

In the picture the little girl beckons to the hen to come to her chickens. This interest in the watchfulness and care of the old hen for her chickens is the mother's instinct. This outgoing of our interest and sympathy is what makes us unselfish. Sharing with others is one of the laws of the kindergarten.There are two ways of sharing with others. We can give and let that be the end of it, and we can give and at the same time give ourselves. The latter is the true giving. Simply giving without putting ourselves in the act is not unselfishness. The greater the sacrifice in the giving, the greater is the value. But too often we lose sight of one point in giving. It is sometimes just as gracious to receive as it is to give. It is better never to give than to give with a patronizing manner.

The child participates in the form of the Divine Activity when he gives himself to his fellow beings. Self-abnegation and devotion to others is

---

[3] Shakespeare, *Julius Caesar*, Act 1 Scene 2

[4] *Froebel Gifts*

necessary to our happiness. God's happiness lies in the fact that he gives himself in creation. He lavishes himself upon us in nature. "The gift without the bearer is bare."[5]

The mother who understands her child wins his confidence and obedience. But to understand him she must live his life with him. The child who has implicit faith in his mother will do as she directs him because it is her wish that he should. As he grows older he will see that his mother tells him to do certain things because it is right that he should, and not simply because it is her will.

There are times when it is impossible to make children do as they should through love, persuasion or by any means except enforcement. Enforcement can be used without violating Froebel's laws.

In this song Froebel's main points are reflection in nature and unselfishness.

In Beckon to the Pigeons the teachings in the main are the same as in Beckon to the chickens. The motto of the Pigeons Song teaches that the mother should seek to find out the cravings of her child and what will satisfy them. The Pigeons Song is the counterpart of the Chicken Song.

The Pigeon song also brings out the value of consistency. Froebel shows how the joyful child life attracts the life of nature, particularly the life of *birds*. He explains it by the fact that children and animals have a point in common, and that is consistency. In the language of both, children and animals "word and fact, fact and word, word and deed, deed and word, are always one and the same."[6]

---

[5] Possible reference from *Froebel Gifts*

[6] [6] Ibid

Mowing Grass Song

"Nothing is more dangerous to the health of the intellect, nothing is more prejudicial to the culture of the heart, than the habit of looking at particular objects and events in detachment from the great whole of life,"[7] are the words of Froebel in his commentary of the Mowing Grass Song. The object of this song is to teach the child that through activity everything in life is related—that is, all of life is so bounded together that everything depends upon something else.

Life is a process. Process implies relationship, and to think of either brings before us the idea of dependency. They go hand in hand. We cannot separate the little events of life from the greater ones for life is a unity.Whether the events be of little or great importance they are not to be ignored for they help to make up a process the great process of life.

Such is the relationship of life that our health of today depends upon our care of it in the past: Our life has its effect upon some other lives, for no one lives for himself alone. So it is all through life. It is all connected.

We are the product of our epoch, our race, and our environment. These are the three factors of which we are the product.

When food is given to a child we should as often as possible explain to him the series of conditions which must exist before that food can become what it is. This is one way of showing the child connection between objects and acts. The result of this knowledge is also an actual physical benefit to the child for the following reason. When he is made to understand something of the

---

[7] *Froebel Gifts*

process by which his food becomes what it is he will naturally see one point in the process more clearly than all the rest, because it will affect him directly, that is the satisfying of his appetite. At first this is the only reason he knows for eating, but when he has learned something of the process by which that food became what it was, he will see that the aim of that process is his physical benefit. The mere act of consuming his food will mean more to him. He will understand why he should eat slowly and masticate his food well.

It will further engender a feeling of thankfulness when he feels that he is depending on his mother, the mower, the cow, the milkmaid, and the baker for his bread and milk, and most of all upon his heavenly Father who sends the rain and sunshine which make the cattle and grass grow. Through this feeling of thankfulness the child will want to serve others in return for the blessings given him.

In no phase of the child's life should the law of unity be violated. In all his mental training there should be logical thought. In all branches of study, history and mathematics especially, the facts are all connected. They come under the law of unity. It is often the case that while one parent corrects a child, the other will shield. This is surely a violation of the law of unity.

We so often make the mistake of judging a person by present conditions. One pupil may outshine another. Of course he deserves praise for his success, but in giving him the praise for his success, let us not always blame the unsuccessful one. Look into the past and judge from the faithful efforts of the unsuccessful one. Faithfulness deserves some reward. We cannot judge rightly unless we know the past conditions.

The kindergarten is not carried on in a haphazard way. It is based on the law of unity. The value of the gifts and occupations lies in the connected thought carried through them.

There are many reasons why we should not look at things just as we see them at the present time without looking back or beyond. Our departed friends and nature in the spring are illustrations. It is necessary to the human life to sacrifice the life of lower animals.Children should not be allowed to see the killing of animals because they would see in it only an act of cruelty and they would be shocked by it. They do not understand that the animals were given to us for food, and that they do not suffer by being killed.

If children are encouraged to imitate the activities of their elders they will understand them more readily. They would then learn through their own experiences something of the process of nature. It would teach them unselfishness, usefulness, and give them an interest in their fellow beings.

As a child often gets his ideals from his literature, he should not be allowed to read just anything which come at hand. His literature should be carefully selected and mapped out for him.

In the picture a little boy is sitting beside a tree. By the trunk of the tree we see it started life with grand prospects. Its general appearance warns us that we should be careful not to graft what is base or false upon an originally noble nature. If this warning is not heeded we must expect a stunted character. Good principles must be grafted.

The little girl sits beside a blighted tree. The meaning of this is that the girl may be spoiled by frivolities. Her life might have been a noble and beautiful one, but instead the tree has been lopped of its top. Nature is the glass by which we see ourselves.

Mutter Und Koselieder

The Mutter Und Koselieder consists of fifty-two songs.These are divided into three groups.The first is an idea of relationship to nature. The second is relationship to man. The third is the relationship of the known to the unknown, that is knowing God and our duty to Him.

We can make another division of the book.In this division we classify the songs in two different groups. The first group may be classed as the songs of relationships; the songs of the second group are those of self-expression.

There has been still a different division made of this book of songs. In this classification there are four groups. The first includes all the songs before the Target Song; the second is from the Target Song to the Light Song; the third is from the Light to the Knights Song; the fourth includes the balance.

The Mutter Und Koselieder is a study of child life.It teaches the importance of the plays of children and how to direct them in order to meet certain needs of their life; and it also seeks a means to satisfy the cravings of child nature.

The acorn buried in the darkness of the earth contains all the power of the mighty oak, so the child in the darkness of unconsciousness possesses all of life potentially. He begins life with all its latent powers.

Froebel's object in writing Mutter Und Koselieder was to present life to the child in ideal form. He realized the importance of the first few years of the child's life.Children are great imitators and because of their desire to reproduce things he gave them these little plays.The advantage of presenting ideals as Froebel has given them is that the child reproduces the experiences for himself which makes them realistic to him. The essence of ideals is a manifestation of God.

The songs of Mutter Und Koselieder contain all the philosophy of education. What is philosophy? It is finding the harmony of things. There seem to be contradictions of harmony all through life. Discords are to be found in all conditions of life. Where is the harmony in life? If we fail to see the harmony it is our own fault, and we cause the discord because we do not understand or see things in their proper relationships. If we would know the harmony of life we must see life in its proper relationships.

For this very reason Froebel sets before the child his ideal relationships through the mother. The sympathetic side of the child's nature is a strong one, and he will strive after an ideal which appeals to his sympathy.This side of his nature can be touched easily through symbols. We use the symbolic method of teaching the child because of his relationship to nature.

If one child is held up as an example of all that is good to another instead of our producing the good effect desired, in all probability the one child will be disliked by the others.Give him object lessons in nature. Let him visit a family of birds.Let him see the loving care of the mother bird and the dependence of the little ones. Point out to him the fact that she knows all the wants of her baby birds and never fails in her ministrations. Such a lesson in nature will appeal to him strongly and will teach him the relationship between him and his mother. Most of his relationships in nature can be taught through nature.

Such is the unity of life that we can interpret the part by the whole. We know the beginning by the end. When we see the seed planted in the earth we know the end of its development. The end is invisible to those who see only the beginning. We must read development backward. In order to appreciate the baby's life and know its needs we must know life as a whole.It is not enough that our knowledge should be limited to the few short years of infancy, if we would further the development of the child. As we see the whole of life, the potentialities of the child will be in proportion to our view of life. If we have the highest ideals of life generally, the little experiences of life will be interpreted proportionally.

"There is no great and no small To the Soul who maketh all."[8]

---

[8] Emerson

It was upon this principle that Froebel wrote this book. Everything in life from the beginning to the end is of such importance that nothing can be considered small. When the first years of the child's life are neglected and the experiences of his little life are considered of no account, it is through ignorance of life as a whole.The value of the beginning means everything. As the child is developed the aftermath will be.

The great truths of life are contained in the book of songs. Its great value lies in the fact it presents the great truths of life in a simple way to the child.

Second Series of the Mother-Plays

The Target Song begins the Second Series of the Mother Plays Songs. The children on the Tower ends this series. The prominent feature of all the preceding songs has been the exhibition of force. Another important feature of the first series is that of relationship. The elementary experiences of the preceding songs are time, space and movement.

In the preceding songs the child advanced from unconsciousness to consciousness. He looked at the life of his little world as a matter of fact. When he gradually became conscious of things around him, he classified only by means of number, form, and size.

With the Target begins a consciousness of an external world. The child begins to classify in this outside diversity. Here the Target begins an advance. Now definite thoughts are coming to the child. He has advanced from the baby age to the kindergarten age.

The underlying idea of all the songs of the second series is proportion. Proportion is number implied in space. As virtue is to character so is proportion to space. When we speak of virtue we mean all the qualities in a proper proportion. It is really proportionate activity-that is, well balanced activities. Virtue carried to excess may become a vice. Self-preservation is a proper thing-is really a virtue-but when carried too far it becomes selfishness.

The underlying idea of this group is illustrated in each song. In the Target Song harmony is the idea produced. In the Pat-a-cake the perfect proportion of parts is the idea. The Birds nest is another illustration of proportion. The Flower basket is an expression of love. In the Pigeon-house the proportion of growth is the underlying idea. The Family Songs, or finger plays close this series.

Kicking Song

This song teaches of the lowest form of development and that is the physical.The kicking song suggests the general type of all efforts to foster activity. This song and the following one are the prototypes of all the Mother Plays. In the kicking song two facts confront the child. He must learn the outer or physical world and the inner or spiritual world. The first development of the child comes through his five senses. It is through the senses that he learns about the outer world.

In this song a process is revealed by which energy is incited. As the child strikes out with his arms and kicks about with his feet, the mother if she be a conscious one will foster these impulsive movements in order to exercise his strength, and to cultivate his activity. The object of this is that through self-activity the child may be led to self-knowledge. The child first discovers that he is when he realizes that he has the power of moving.

This special little play with the limbs is an illustration of a great truth. The mother's object in this game is to develop power. She uses the game as a point of departure in education. Froebel says "foster the child's activity and it will rise to productive energy."[9] He argues that if the mind controls the body, the body can be made to act upon the mind. As the mother goes on with the play, she sings and making rhythmic movements with the limbs, reveals her love through the melody of her voice.

The action of the mind and the body go hand and hand, and the rhythmic movement of the limbs with the mother's voice acts upon the child's mind. In

---

[9] *Froebel Gifts*

this way physical power is developed and thought is regulated. Although the baby understands not a word the mother says he knows through this play all opposition is sent by love.

Man is only what he makes himself. For this reason he should study methods by which energy may be guided and developed. A sense of power must be awakened and a love of exertion created in the child for power not used weakens. As an illustration of this we have the Dodder plant which has depended so long on other plants for life that now it has no root of its own. Another illustration that unused power weakens is the hermit crab. In the beginning the hermit crab was like other crabs.He had a hard shell and all means of caring for himself, but he thought he would like to inhabit the cast off shells of other crabs until he is no longer capable of taking care of himself.

The growth of energy through opposition is a general law. It is by opposing possibilities that, character is formed. The mother presses her hand against the baby's kicking feet.In the old myth Hercules strangles while in his cradle the serpents which *attack* him. We very often take obstacles away from children when we should let them overcome them.The child should be left alone to struggle reasonably in order to develop his manliness. To develop his intellect we must not make the path of knowledge too smooth for him. To develop his moral qualities he should deal with moral problems. He who cannot learn upon himself must lean upon others and so becomes like the Dodder plant or the Hermit Crab.

The motto of this song teaches that all life manifests itself in action. The baby shows by his movements how full of life he is, and through this movement his inner life strengthens. The vitality shown in his movements is a revelation of God. The instinctive response of the mother in this game with the limbs is a hint from heaven that she is to enrich the inner life. The child comes into the world with fine sentiments and *foreshadowing* of truths which need only the external occasion to awaken.

The amount of vitality of the child is shown by his activity. Through this activity his inner life is strengthened, and then he begins to imitate. His activity reaches a state where he produces different things he sees in his little world. He wants to investigate and discover the meaning of the world around him.

When we speak of presentments or foreshadowing of truth, we mean the child has only the possibility of the idea. When we speak of definite thought we mean the child has potentialities which must be developed.

It is necessary that the child should have definite movement, because it is in this way he has definite thought. The instinctive mother loves to talk and sing to her child. So often the mother accompanies her little games with a song. In this way the child connects sounds with ideas, therefore it is well for the child to be talked to often. The connection between words and objects should be pointed out to him.The melody of the mother's voice and her words have also a moral effect upon the child. The child learns to know his mother's voice. It calms and attracts him, yet he does not understand a word. He later learns to obey that voice and it appeals to him. The emotion of the child is stirred by the mother's voice.

The definite movement of this game tends to produce definite thought. If the movement is indefinite the idea will be indefinite to the child.

Froebel teaches that the child must develop through obstacles as the race has done. So the child must overcome oppositions that he may have a stronger character. We value anything ever so much more if we get it by overcoming some obstacle. Then like Hercules teach the child to begin to overcome in his cradle the serpents which attack him through life. In our efforts to encourage his energies we must not carry the child too far. If he is expected to do the impossible he may become discouraged. From his small successes he will gain a desire for larger ones.

The ulterior purpose of the child's energy is for himself. If he sees that he is giving pleasure to his mother and others by his actions, that itself will return to him as a blessing.

Love is said to increase with the development of its object. As the child is the object of the mother's love, that love will increase as the child fulfills all the mother's hopes.

The child feels a power within him by his movements. As he advances he should be taught to see an outside force. Stir the child's imagination and let him see the living, loving force in nature. Froebel teaches that life is a unity, and the principle of over coming belongs not only to childhood but all through life.

In the picture the stream has been dammed that its force may turn the mill wheel. The boy has set his toy mill in the stream. One boy watches the toy and tries to understand it. The little girl wades with bare feet in the water and kneads the sand into dough. Each child shows a different individuality by the same fascination. The general thought of the picture is that if force is not constrained it wastes itself.

All life is connected from childhood plays to the serious experiences of manhood.

"He has not learned a lesson of life who does not each day surmount a fear."[10]

---

[10] Attributed to Ralph Waldo Emerson, 1803-1882

Weathervane Song

In the Kicking Song the child discovered a moving power within himself. In the Weathervane he learns about an external force.

The first truth emphasized in this song is the relation of cause and effect. Froebel teaches that the child is educated through imitation. The act of imitation proves that the child has become conscious of his own power to originate movements, and that he voluntarily exercises this power. The child sees a moving force in the outside world, and he assimilates it and reproduces it through imitation. Assimilation is comprehension. The child has reached a stage of wanting to understand things he sees, and it is through imitation that he satisfies this investigative spirit.

In the Kicking Song the child discovered himself and a moving force within. In the Weathervane he discovers the outer world and its motive force. The second point brought out in this song is imitation.The act of imitation is the first sure sign of the beginning of will power.

The motive of the kicking game is the solicitation of force, and is followed by the Weathervane as it is intended to influence the activity of imitation. A cause is said to be worth a whole series of effects.Unless the child through imitation can get some idea of the cause the effect means little to him. The child who imitates has formed an ideal and he is using his energy to understand it. He has discovered an energy to be the cause of a perceptible effect. This is the beginning of his intellectual freedom.

The two ideas of all education are assimilation and reproduction. Absolute reproduction is not the highest form. Relative reproduction is the highest and that is when the child catches the idea in the spirit.

It is not enough that the child should be satisfied with the external. He should be trained to go back to the spirit. At this first stage of reasoning languages are born. Lower animals do not talk because they do not reason and therefore have nothing to say.

At this imitative stage of development the child should be protected from hearing or seeing things which we would not want him to reproduce. For since each activity helps to form the character it is obvious that what the child imitates he will tend to become.

Plato says that the first school of the soul is the "school of astonishment," and that the "beginning of knowledge is in wonder."[11]

The reason that wind is an appropriate object here is that it excites wonder. The phenomena of storms inspire fear to the unaccustomed soul, but the phenomena of wind inspire pure and simple wonder. The child finds himself in a presence of a world in movement. He feels its breath and hears its voice. All children think that moving objects cause wind. The only movement he knows anything of is self-movement.He knows that he moves himself and naturally thinks that the Weathervane and trees move of their own accord.

It is an intellectual crisis when the child first discovers that his first theory of the wind is false, and that the wind is not the effect but rather the cause. Speculation with regard to the nature of the unseen energy of the wind begin to occupy the mind and the child is eager to know what the wind is and what makes it.

The mystery of the wind may be traced in myths.Wind gods appear in all mythologies.

Great care should be taken in answering the child's questions about the wind. In Froebel's commentary when the child questions about the wind he is not answered, but pointed to another mystery. Here avoid the pedantry born of answering masked questions. It has been said that every premature definition of virtue is the seed of vice. So our premature answers might kill some seed of thought.

Why the Weathervane so closely follows the Kicking Song is evident. The

---

[11] Plato, 424 B.C.E.

19

kicking game is a process by which energy is incited. The child learned of a force within him. In the Weathervane he discovered an outside force and began to see that there is a cause behind the moving Weathervane. If there is a cause behind one moving object there must be a cause behind all. This is the beginning of his knowledge of the unity of nature and of the One who is the cause of all creation.

Falling, Falling Song

Every mother instinctively plays games with her child. She does it in answer to her child's needs. This instinct suggests an educational principle. The very fact that fairy-tales and certain games have been used in all ages shows that they are the outward clothing of a truth. In the Kicking Song the necessity of overcoming obstacles is strongly brought out. The child then discovered the ego-I am. He also discovered the external world.

The three relationships taught in the songs are first the child's relationships to nature, the second is to man, and the third to God. The relations which exist between a mother and her child are instinctive. Through this relationship he learns his relation to God.

The great principle of this song is *that* separation is necessary to consciousness.There must be a breaking up of unconscious unity in order to return to a higher form of union; in other words to a conscious one. As an illustration of this we have the history of the earth. The earth was a conglomerate mass. Then there was a breaking up of that mass into the different divisions of land and water, etc. That was the breaking up of unity for a higher development. Language is another illustration of this principle. That separation is necessary to consciousness.

The word *tribulum* in the Roman Tongue means threshing the floor. The early Christians used the word and meant separating the dross from the gold. After separating ourselves thus from our own English word tribulation in studying its derivation, we come back to it with a deeper appreciation of its meaning.Civil society is another illustration.In the different trades there is unity in variety. A person who stays at home always does not appreciate his home as much as one who leaves it for a while and goes back. Those who are accustomed to seeing nothing but beautiful scenery do not appreciate it as much as others who do not have the same opportunity. If we are continually surrounded by friends we do not know the value of friendship until we find ourselves in the midst of strangers.

As the child grows the physical separation from his mother grows more and more. There is the breaking up of an unconscious unity. This separation should not be allowed to grow too far. There must be a return to a conscious union. In the Falling, Falling Game as the baby falls for the first few times naturally he shows fear and anxiety, but when he is accustomed to it his fear changes to delight.

"Baby well may laugh at harm, While beneath is mother's arm."[12]

Here it is that the child begins to trust his mother. Just from this the mother can begin to make a bond so strong between her, child and herself that it will be a protection all through life to him. Pestalozzi taught that in faith must be sought the point of contact between the nurturing and the nurtured life.[13] Just as the baby in the little falling game learns to trust his mother's arm because it was strong, so must he learn to trust her wisdom and her love. The secret of strength is always the same and the words of the song are a faint echo of "The eternal God is thy refuge, and underneath are the everlasting arms."[14]

This thought has been the strength of heroes in all ages. Pestalozzi teaches that we must love men, trust them, and obey them before we can rise to loving, trusting, and obeying God. He says it is principally through the relations which exist between a mother and her child that we rise to this highest state of love.

Although separation is necessary to consciousness, there is such a thing as separation lasting too long. In this game the baby is not allowed to remain down but is brought back so that he may not forget the first condition. Separation should be temporary only. Entire separation produces forgetfulness.

The best way to teach a child a lesson is by presenting ideals to him. This is

---

[12] Possible reference from *Froebel Gifts*

[13] Johann Heinrich Pestalozzi, 1746–1827, Swiss pedagogue and education reformer

[14] *Deuteronomy* 33:27

one of the offices of the fairy-tale. In the fairy-tales we take the child into an entirely different world.

The mother who sees the principles underlying her instinctive actions with her child will apply these principles all through his life. When the child is cared for and made happy by his mother the first seed of love is sown within him. When she protects him from danger the seed of trust is sown. These germs of love and trust soon develop. These are the first elements of moral development. They are also the elements of religion and it is by faith in his mother that the child rises to faith in God.

The great principle of this song applies to older children as well. When the boy dashes off in some sport let him take the consequences of a fall. It will teach him carefulness. Inattention and weakness must be overcome before the child is able to rule himself. It is sometimes well for children to suffer the consequences of their actions so that they may become masters of themselves.

The various teachings of this song are first the development of the dawning sense of self; separation is necessary to consciousness; separation persisted in defeats its own end; a conscious union from physical dependence to spiritual sympathy.

In Froebel's commentary of the song he repeats that the child shall fall with sufficient force to experience a slight shock. He must feel that he is slipping away from his mother. Then as she draws him back again he feels that a loving power watches over his fall and makes it safe. Life is a series of falls. The history of man is to fall and to rise from his fall. The drama of history and the drama of infancy begin with the fall.

All's Gone Song

The All's Gone Song treats of an absence of a thing. Just as in the Weathervane a present fullness is shown so in the All's Gone a present lack is shown. In the imitation of the Weathervane the child controls the origin of the cause of an effect and for this reason he enters into the little play with great enjoyment and seriousness. He feels a power within himself and unconsciously experiences the fact that a moving force causes an object to move. From this in a short while his natural conclusion will be that there is a moving force behind living objects and this will be the final step to the knowledge of the one great Power of all created things.

The mother talks to the child about his supper being gone, tells his cheeks to grow rosy, his lips, his flesh to grow firm because they have been fed. By this the child knows he ate his supper for a cause. Then vaguely at first, but with increasing clearness the child learns to connect his food with his bodily health and growth. By this connection he gets his first idea of the mystery of change.When the mother tells the child the food will make him grow he knows it will take time for this to be accomplished.He begins to see that effect does not always immediately follow a cause.

A child cannot begin too soon to learn this as it is necessary to his health, his intellect and his morality. Children will do things which are *detrimental* to their health because they cannot see any immediate effect. They should be taught that in life causes are mediated. The fact that evil associations corrupt good manners cannot be realized by the child until he is taught the law of mediation. It is only in the magic world that causes are done away with.

The chief thing taught in the Weathervane Song is the law of the relation of cause and effect. The child will begin life with a wrong idea if he is allowed to think that an effect comes always immediately after a cause. In the Weathervane there is a presence of a great power. In All's Gone is shown that the first cause is mediated by a succession of causes.

Mothers naturally play these little games with their children. The Falling Game teaches that childhood must be grounded in faith. The All's gone game gives explanation to that which seems to be a destructive process. So all the plays contain great truths whether the mother is conscious of the results or not.

Two other ideas contained in this song are change and time. Time is an original suggestion of the mind. When the baby looks into his empty plate, he knows that it contained his suppers a while ago and from this he connects the past with the present. Something which was is contrasted with something which is not. Here he recognizes a change. The power of motion, sympathy and imitation the child shares with young animals, but when he has reached the point of recognition of change he enters upon his human career.

Confronted by vanishing objects the child often shows wonder and fear. He wonders where and why the object has gone. He does not know whether it will come back or not. Here we realize that the child is having his first struggle with the great problem which has puzzled the mind of man in all historic development. This is only the beginning of an experience which he will have all through life. His mind will be perplexed by the mysteries in life as long as he is in the world.

There are two classes of change brought out in the marginal picture. There is a connection between the moral lesson of the picture and the baby's vanishing supper. Baby's supper returns in his rosy cheeks and his sturdy limbs. As his supper returns so does his deed. The picture clearly presents a fact of disappearance. The supper, the birds, the slice of bread all disappear. The return of the supper is a certain outcome, which is shown in the baby's physical development. The outcome of heedlessness and want of consideration shown in the picture is destruction. When the child is able to recognize change he begins to observe a return of his deeds. In the child's mind the food is destroyed to make his body. In the picture everything disappears and the scene is changed.

The child has not yet experienced the consequences of gratifying his impulses. So it has not occurred to him to consider the consequences of his actions in any way.

We give the child crude experiences because his mind is not developed enough for any other kind.

There are three classes of change. The first is that which is produced by outside influence.Rocks are worn away by water; water is turned into ice; there is destruction by fire. The second form of change is both within the thing itself and without. To this form belong plant and animal life. In the third form of change external influence has nothing to do. To this class, the change of character belongs. The surroundings cannot make the character altogether. If the character is to be anything at all most of its making must come from within.

Although the idea of time is an original one, a sense of its relations must be developed. Show the child the relationship of yesterday to today. Call his mind to something which is past in contrast to the present.

Since "good is conquered evil,"[15] we learn what is right by finding out what is wrong. It is of great importance to hold up to the imagination of children noble deeds. So many traditional tales bring out the virtues of the hero by contrast with bad people. This is good for the child. He likes to imitate and if he is given high ideals the good in him will be brought out by the beauty of the ideal. Not only in literature should the ideals be given him, but in everything brought to bear upon his character. We must not make the mistake of presenting ideals for which the mind is not prepared.

One special reason why we should present ideals to the child is to develop a motive power within him. In this way he will learn to do the right because it is right. When the child is conscious of his motives his moral life begins. Appeal to the child's sympathy, kindness and generosity. Teach him to make conscious ideals and obey them.

The child should not be allowed to see a thing just as it is and be satisfied

---

[15] Possible reference from *Romans* 12:21

with that. He must be taught to trace the relationship of cause and effect. This will lead him to attach a moral quality to his actions. Train him to connect the past with the present, that is the history of things. He must see things in all their relationships. This will lead him to reason logically and not remain satisfied with just what he can see. When he has been trained in this respect he will begin to attribute a moral effect to his actions and from this will learn self-restraint and consideration for others. Our aim in giving the child high ideals and developing his moral qualities is to arm him for life. If we incite him to noble warfare his character will be stronger than if we continually shield him. Our aim is to arm the child not guard him. He should be given the power to guard himself.

Tick Tack Song

In the All's Gone Song the child had an experience of time in the present and the past. In the Tick-tack he learns the value of time. We know time to be an original suggestion of the mind, but the measurement and value must be taught. It is necessary to teach the child to do things at the proper time because the harmony of life depends upon it. The importance of order and punctuality in all the relationships of life must be taught.

The irresistible charm of the clock for the child can be made the point of educating him so that he will carefully consider, understand, and use time to the best advantage. To the child time may seem to be a taskmaster. If the clock is used as a means of education, he will not think of time is such a way. He will understand that by doing things at the proper time he will be happier. He will see that he is free by the obedience to the law of time. Procrastinators are the slaves of time. Time is always their master. When the time comes for pleasure they cannot have it because there is some neglected task to be done.

The attraction of the pendulum for the child is known by everybody. The reason of this is that any mystery quickens the imaginations and the pendulum is a mystery to the child. It is also a rhythmic movement. The child is born into a world of rhythm, and it would be strange indeed if he gave no sign of being in harmony with the universal rhythm. That the child is in harmony with the universal rhythm is shown by the nursery games as Pat-a-cake and any of the little games where there is a rhythmic movement, and the songs which lull him to sleep. It is no wonder that the child wants to know what the clock says. Froebel has used the clock as a rhythmic call to lead a rhythmic life. It tells the child what time to get up in the morning; it tells him there is a time for him to eat; there is a time to play and a time to sleep.

Out of the unconsciousness of the child will grow the consciousness of his daily life as he understands the measurements of time. What good result can come from this song of the clock? Order has been said to be heaven's first law and if the principles of this song are carried out the child will be made orderly. Froebel's idea is to show the child the importance and beauty of order. When the child is being taught to have a time for everything his mind is being prepared for logical thinking. By showing the child the importance of being punctual we teach him to be unselfish, for to be tardy is to be inconsiderate for others.

In the picture of this song the child wants his mother to show him a picture. She tells him it is time for his bath and points to the kitten which is smoothing her fur as if expecting afternoon visitors. She reminds the child that father will soon be home and will want to see his baby neat and clean. So the child has been denied a pleasure of seeing the picture to teach him self-denial. The very idea of giving pleasure to his father has made the act of punctuality one of consideration.

Froebel brings in the song a suggestion of cleanliness. There is a tie between punctuality and cleanliness. Punctuality is order in time. Cleanliness is order in space. From the thought of cleanliness rises the thought of a clean heart. Froebel has also connected orderly activity with spiritual purity. This connection is seen in the fact when a person has allowed himself to be late in keeping an engagement.

Everything goes wrong in the haste to get off and the person becomes nervous and fretful. When the day is started in such a way one is upset for the rest of the day. There is no order in anything, only tumult. When we are reminded of these common place facts we realize the importance of the clock for a rhythmic life. "Time is the eternal flight from the alone to the alone."[16]

---

[16] *Froebel Gifts*

Taste Song

Taste is the first sense developed. It is through the senses that the child learns the outer world. It has been said that the mouth is the center of psychic life. Taste is the first sense to yield clear perceptions to which memory is attached. Often very young children will make wry faces at sight of medicine, showing that they remember an earlier sensation of taste. The fact that young children carry every thing to their mouths shows that they want to find out something about the thing.

The senses have a double office. They are a channel through which external nature speaks, and an avenue revealing the spirit. The spirit of nature speaks to the spirit of the child. The spirit of the world speaks to us through our senses, mainly through the sense of sight. Colors will affect us in different ways; beautiful scenery, different kinds of weather, music each has some effect on us.

Froebel has made the special point in his Taste song to be true aesthetic culture. In this little play the mother puts into the child's mouth in succession a plum, a piece of apple, and an almond and leads him to discriminate their several savors. The mother seeks by the child's reflecting upon his experience to have him gain a mental as well as a physical pleasure. Sweetness tells him he should not eat too much of it. Sourness tells him that in many cases it is unripe and should not be eaten. The educational points of this song are the conscious exercise of the power of comparison, and the suggestion that all objects have their own language. It is necessary to the child's development that we teach him to understand the language of the senses and listen to what they teach. He can be made to see the indolence which follows gluttony etc. The warnings of taste and smell are reinforced by warnings to other senses. The apple's greenness and hardness tell the same story as its sourness. The melancholy hues of many poisonous plants confirm the suggestion of their repellent odors. The child should be trained to use his senses to find out the real nature of objects.

If physical pleasure is unaccompanied by mental enjoyment, the effect will be the decrease of the desire for the physical and an increase for the mental.

New books, new scenes give opportunity for mental actions. The senses should be a means not the end by which the soul grows. We should eat to live, but we should not live to eat.

"Sensation is a mental condition resultant upon physical contact. Perception is the step following the sensation in which the mind attributes sensation to its proper source."[17]

The senses have different ranks according to their nature. We must agree upon a certain basis to classify things. The senses are inclusive or exclusive, inward or otherwise, and destructive or otherwise. Touch is included is all the other senses. Touch is exclusive therefore it is ranked low. Taste is exclusive. It is also destructive. Food must be destroyed to be tasted. Taste is not as general a sense as touch. Smell is higher than either touch or taste, because it is inclusive.Hearing is inclusive. Sight is higher than hearing because light waves travel faster than sound. Sight is the highest sense. The organ of sight has been called the window of the soul.

As so many words have a double meaning so has taste. It has another meaning beside the physical. Since Froebel seeks in this song to lay the foundation of an aesthetic education we must begin where the child stands and gradually lead him to a higher plane. It has been said that no child whose organ of hearing is normally developed is absolutely unmusical. One of the best ways to cultivate the hearing of little children is by directing attention to the sounds of nature. Nothing is more beautiful than nature, and since it is a part of our aim to cultivate the aesthetic side of the child we might begin

---

[17] Possible reference from *Froebel Gifts*

with the songs of birds, the voices of the wind, the babble of the playful brook, and the splash of the waves. There is a relation between music and emotion, and noble feelings may be aroused by correspondent melodies and rhythms.If the child learns melodies and rhythms from nature he will get only those of freedom and joy which he should only know.

The training of sense is an important thing, because the brain is the center of all sensation, and the brain structures are the product of mental activity. Give the child the best whether it concerns his seeing, hearing, touching or smelling.We can only learn to love the beautiful by creating the beautiful. We must not pervert the child's aesthetic sense by giving him ugly pictures and ugly toys. But we must not forget that all true beauty unifies strength and simplicity.

Physically we taste only that which we are beginning to *assimilate* or make over into our own organism, and the same is true spiritually. Our souls become noble or base, fair or foul, as we prefer the noble or base, the fair or the foul in life, manners, literature, and art. Our genuine attractions and repulsions define our characters. When we realize this we will understand that the cultivations of taste is an important phase of education.

Froebel's aim was to make the child master of himself.He is not satisfied with giving children simple food, beauties of nature, and the best of everything in our power, but he would have them choose it. He would have them self-restraining. He is not content when the motive of self-restraint in faith and the mother or others, but rather the self-coercion because of an inwardly compelling ideal.

The Pigeon House

Before any system of education can be determined upon it is necessary to know the nature of the mind. German philosophy teaches in this respect that all of man's development is a procession from the lowest to the highest. The lowest form of nature comes from the same source as man himself. He may see himself reflected in nature as in a looking glass. The best way to know himself is to look out into the world and separate himself from himself. We had an illustration of this in the Falling Game that is that separation is necessary to consciousness.

That was the physical separation. Now we come to the mental separation. Intellectually and physically this separation must take place. It should not be the end but rather the means. When the child is mentally independent of the parent the bond of union is stronger between them than before. A closer fellowship exists then. Separation for a higher union is the typical thought of the Pigeon House game. The pigeons return after their flights and in their house talk to each other.

The idea of pigeons talking to each other would please a child, and he would be the more ready to tell all he had seen during the day if inspired by this little lesson in nature. The going out in the day time and the return of the pigeons at night symbolize the family to the child. It is a tendency of the child's mind to be interested in masked forms of stories.

This law of separation is operative all through life. It is illustrated in the philosophy of life, in our language, in racial development, and in civil society. We are living in an era of combination.

The typical thought of this song is applied educationally as a symbol. The child goes out for his little journeys, and like the pigeons returns with his series of experiences. The mother should never be too busy to listen to her child's experiences. Nothing should be too trivial for her attention. We present great truths of life to the child by symbols. In this way he is separated from the thing itself and consequently gets the truth more forcibly.

If the child is not encouraged to reflect after his observation his experiences may mean very little to him. Reflection and observation of experiences are brought out in The Children on the Tower. This is the stage of life when the mother lose her, child if she has no other bond than a physical one. The only way she can hold him is by sympathy and love. Communion with her child means everything.

Another important idea of the Pigeon House song is that we see ourselves in nature. In this song the going out and the return of the pigeons symbolize to the child his own little adventure into the world even from the nursery. Froebel teaches that that which characterizes baby's life must characterize all life.

The child craves separated truths. Mother Goose is based upon *worldwide* myths. They are pictures of the world framed by the human mind. Children instantly grasp these ideas.

This song is connected with The Weathervane by the fact that the child is looking back for causes all the time. It connects with The Fishes in that he sees himself in nature. The laws of nature are the laws of man and they work together.

The Fish in the Brook

The motto of this song teaches that activity of any kind is attractive to a child. The child regards with new delight each living thing he sees because this element of activity is the same in him. Life attracts life. The child finds pleasure in his mechanical toys, but it is not as great an enjoyment as he finds in living objects such as fish and birds. The origin of the movement of the animal is what attracts him.

The force of the activity comes from within and is therefore on a higher plane than that of his toy. A fish or a bird has even more attraction for the child than a cat or a dog. The reason of this is the freedom of the fish and bird. Gravitation rules our freedom and that of the cat and dog but not the fish and bird. The child is a creature of activity, and the highest forms of activity in animals attract him for this very reason. It is well for the child to spend much time with animals, for in them he finds comrades indeed, and through their companionship knows himself better.

A fish out of water cannot live. If the fish which had always lived in cold waters should go into warm waters it would die. The little girl in the picture has insisted on having a fish taken out of the water. All the attraction is gone and she is amazed.

So it is with human creatures. Take them out of their element and they are unhappy.If a person who had always lived with educated, cultured, refined people should suddenly have for his companion coarse, illiterate people he would not be contented; or should the case be reversed unhappiness would exist.

The element in which a child lives affects his pleasures. He should live in a pure atmosphere. The little world in which he lives should be one of purity and all that is good and noble. Children are great imitators, and their whole nature may be changed by the atmosphere of the world in which they live.

There are two factors in movement which affect the child's pleasure. The degree of his pleasure depends upon the degree of the freedom of the movement, and upon the source of the movement. A child finds pleasure in pulling his toy wagon and his train of cars. He enjoys riding a stick for a horse, but how much more pleasure he finds in the real horse for there he finds life and the source of the movement comes from within the animal. The greater the degree of freedom in the movements of the animal, the greater the attraction. This explains the boy's love for a kite although the kite is an inanimate thing.The freedom as it sails and darts through the air appeals to the activity of the boy.

There is a difference between freedom and license. The highest degree of freedom comes from within. License is lawlessness. Freedom is living according to law. We gain freedom by observing certain rules. What would become of our health if we did not observe certain laws. Nothing will tie us down more surely than ill health. To obey the civil authority means our freedom. Rulers in our daily life are necessary. If we would accomplish anything we must conform to certain rules. What would our education be if we paid no attention to rules. Knowledge is power and power is freedom.

Freedom of movement in the physical world is symbolic not only of the child's physical nature, but of his mental as well. The student of today spends a great deal of time in the gymnasium for his physical development. Our bodies are trained in order to give us control over them. So must our mental nature be controlled.The child's mind must be trained in a logical way.

The standpoints of the development of the child should be controlled by free movement. The source of the child's actions should come from within. The highest form of activity is self-activity. That means "That not merely shall the learner do all himself; not merely that he shall be benefited by what he himself does; it implies that at all times he himself shall be active; that the activity should enlist his entire self in all the phases of being; it would have all that is in the child self-active-by growing simultaneously and continuously."[18]

The best way to get a child to act is to appeal to an ideal in him. If the right thing cannot be accomplished by this means then authority should be exercised. In exercising authority over children convictions should be in accordance with universal law. By universal law we mean those which have always existed and have never changed. When governing children we should not use our authority simply because we have the power to do so.

There are different ways of possessing. We may have the material possession or we may have the spiritual possession. When the little girl saw the fish in the brook she wanted it out of the water so that she could get it, but when she had it in her possession she was not satisfied. It was not the material thing she wanted. The attraction was all in the swimming, gliding, and darting. Only the spiritual possession satisfied her. The highest form of possession is the spiritual. A successful though, a simple life is an illustration of this point. A successful life does not always consist of material possessions. One may view some beautiful scenery and not own one small part of it. He finds great pleasure in it and is glad of the privilege. He has a spiritual possession.

Environments mean much. So it is very important that children should select good companions, good books, and the best of everything that is possible for them to have.

In this song Froebel has pointed out how essential it is that children should know the distinction between crooked and straight in a metaphorical sense. He has shown how important it is that we should plant in the hearts of children "a love for all that is straight-forward in thought, word, and deed, and a hatred for whatever violates this ideal."[19] The effect of this teaching will be an active, joyful, and free life like that of the fish and the bird.

---

[18] Possible reference from *Froebel Gifts*

[19] *Froebel Gifts*

The Kindergarten

The first years of the child's life are very important ones. It is then that the child is being influenced most strongly by his surroundings. The young child's mind is easily impressed.The education of the young child is considered by many of no importance. The first few years of his life from an educational standpoint are neglected in many cases. The question as to whether it is right or not to send children to kindergarten is often raised. The objection in some cases is that the child's mind is taxed at too tender an age.

Whether that comes from ignorance of the Froebelian methods or not is not for us to say. But when we consider that influences are being brought to bear every day upon the child's mind we do say that no harm can come from a logical training of his mental powers although he is little more than an infant. He is being educated in some way whether we would have it so or not.

What do we mean by education? According to Spencer, education is complete living.It is well for us to keep clearly in view that in our methods of education complete living is the end to be achieved. If this is kept in mind subjects and methods of instruction will be selected with reference to this end. In estimating the respective values of information which will be useful in after life Spencer says "Our first step must obviously be to classify, in the order of their importance, the leading kinds of activity which constitute human life."[20]

Often parents do not realize the importance of that "spontaneous educa-tion"[21] which goes on in early years. The child's keen observation is considered

---

[20] Herbert Spencer, 1820-1903, English Philosopher and Sociologist

[21] Possible reference to techniques of Maria Montessori, 1870-1952, Physician and Educator

restlessness and is ignored while it should be made as accurate as possible. This need is diligently administered to in the kindergarten, even though it is considered by some people a nursery.

In the kindergarten the child has the advantage of being under the care of one who has theoretic guidance.

In the kindergarten the scope of education includes the body as well as the mind. One cannot be developed as it should be without the other.

As every influence brought to bear upon the child serves as an educational factor let his environment be the very best that we can give him. His whole nature may be changed by the atmosphere of the little world in which he lives.

The child comes into the world with only possibilities, therefore he must be educated. A desire to know the meaning of things which come before him must be created. A knowledge of the child's needs and possibilities, and a study of child nature is necessary to a true educational system. In order to have a standard by which to judge the child we must study the history of the race. "Knowledge is power."[22] In all ages man has been striving for freedom and this he cannot have unless he has power. The development of the race has been by throwing off shackles. The child is helpless and must be guided. It is during childhood that the foundation of the afterlife is laid. In the education of the child we must have the ability to meet his needs.

The aim of education is to train all sides of the child's nature. In developing one side we must not neglect another. He must have an all-round development. His intellect, his will power, his sympathy etc. must be educated.

Froebel does not stand alone in the development of the idea of education, other educators even as far back as Aristotle have set forth the same idea. The kindergarten is one step in a process. It is a step by which to reach a higher one.

Through his own lonely childhood Froebel realized the needs of little children. He lacked sympathetic friends and his childhood has very lonely. Out of this grew the idea of the kindergarten. Children are like primitive man. They cannot grasp the abstract. They must have the object itself.

---

[22] *scientia potentia est, knowledge is power*, phrase attributed to Sir Francis Bacon, 1561–1626

The root principle upon which the kindergarten is built is the law of harmonious development. Only by this law can harmony be produced. There are certain laws under which we all must live. This is an important thing for the child to learn. He must be trained to see why he should conform to certain rules. Teach him to see the reason why there should be such a thing as law. When he has learned this he will see that in order to be free he must be obedient to law. One of the first laws to be taught is that of functionality. The child must also learn his relationships in life. His relationship to his family is naturally the first he learns. Teach him this by object lessons in nature. Children can be taught easily through nature because they have so much in common with it. Froebel's system is based on symbols. In the same way the race was taught.

The gifts and occupations of the kindergarten are the means by which the child produces things. The gift is the thing by which we analyze and synthesize. The child reproduces the gift through the occupation. A safe test of knowledge is reproduction. In the process of education the kindergarten is the first step. For many, as we have said before, it *(Kindergarten)* is thought to be a very plausible but very dangerous educational system. It is thought that there is too much coaxing. The chief aim of the educator is supposed to be that of amusing the child. Contrary to this mistaken idea, the aim of the educator is to incite and guide the child's self-activity.

There is a prevailing idea that the kindergarten is a place to send children where they can be interested and kept out of mischief. True, it is the place to interest the child, but his interest is quickened through the incitement to self-activity. The founder of the kindergarten appeals first then last and always to the self-activity of the child.

Theme on Light

In this single department of natural philosophy we will not enter upon the discussion as to how the groping man arose. We will take him at a certain stage of his development, when, by evolution or sudden endowment, he became possessed of the apparatus of thought and the power of using it. For a time-and that historically a long one-he was limited to mere observation, accepting what nature offered, and confining intellectual actions to it alone. The apparent motions of sun and stars first drew towards them the questioning of the intellect, and accordingly astronomy was the first science developed.

But other objects than the motions of the stars attracted the attention of the ancient world. Light was a familiar phenomenon, and from the earliest times we find men busy with the attempt to account for it. But without experiment, which belongs to a later stage of scientific development, little progress could be made in this subject. Still the ancients did make some progress. They satisfied themselves that light moved in straight lines; they knew also that light was reflected from polished surfaces, and that the angle of incidence of the rays of light was equal to the angle of reflection. These two results of ancient scientific-curiosity-constitute the starting point of the progress made in this branch of science.

Physiologically speaking, light is the sensation of sight.Physically considered, it is that agent which, by its action on the retina of the eye, excites in us the sensation of vision. Two leading hypothesis regarding the nature of light have been propounded, which are totally different in character.

"The light from the sun, the twinkling of the stars, the colors of the rainbow, and the various hues of the floor of nature remain the same as when they gladdened the heart of Noah, but how have the explanation of the phenomena varied!"[23] One is the so-called emission or corpuscular hypothesis which was supported by Descartes (1629), Newton (1672), and most physicists up to the early part of the past century.

It assumes that a luminous body (that is the sun) emits minute material particles (corpuscles) which travel through space in all directions with immense velocity; these particles by their impact upon the nerve-woven retina produce the sensation of sight. As a rose emits minute particles which, reaching the nostrils, enables us to smell the rose, so a star is supposed to emit particles of light which, on reaching the eye, enable us to see the star.

This hypothesis is now discarded by scientists.The theory which obtain at the present time, called the undulatory or wave-theory, is based upon the hypothesis that energy is transmitted from body to body, that is from sun to the earth (and the reverse), in the form of vibrations or wave-action in the all-pervading ether. The evidence of the correctness of any theory is its exclusive confidence to explain and coordinate phenomena. It is not claimed that all phenomena have been fully explained by the wave-theory; the scientists merely claim that all we know at the present time about light is in perfect accord with it. According to the wave-theory, light is that vibration of the ether which may be appreciated by the organ of sight.

That light travels with finite speed was first established in 1676 by the Danish astronomer Olaf-Roemer, then engaged in Paris in observing the eclipses of Jupiter's moons. From the results of these observations it was calculated that light required sixteen minutes and thirty-six seconds to traverse the diameter of the earth's orbit, approximately 185,000,000 miles. The results obtained by Michelson at Cleveland (1882) is that light travels 186,380 miles per second. Notwithstanding its great speed, light requires no less than three years to reach us from the nearest fixed star and from those more distant it requires centuries.

Although the ancients made not great progress in the science of light it was a familiar phenomenon. So was the phenomenon of color familiar to them.

---

[23] reference from *The Principles of Physics* published 1895 by Alfred P. Gage

"This colored world of ours"[24] was theirs also, but they did not attribute color to their phoilius[25], who drove westerly all day in his flaming chariot. They did not know that the bridge, Bifrost, the only access to the sacred Asgard, owed its brilliant colors to the sun. They appreciated its delicate beauty. It was a fantastic sacred thing to them; so much so that they were afraid the frost giants might destroy it and they placed a guard to watch it night and day.

"Bifrost *in the* east shone forth in brightest green;

On its top in snow white sheen, Heimdall all at his post was seen."[26]

Not until after the discovery of the composition of solar light did the rainbow mean what it does now. It is a solar spectrum on a grand scale. It is the result of refraction, total reflection and dispersion of sun-light by falling rain-drops. In the rainbow a new phenomenon was introduced. Descartes discovered the composition of solar light, but for Newton was reserved the enunciation of the true law. Through his celebrated experiment of allowing a thin sunbeam to pass through a closed window-shutter. He pierced an orifice in the shutter, and the beam passing through stamped a round white image of the sun on the opposite wall of the room.

In the path of this beam Newton placed a prism, expecting to see the image of the sun, after refraction still round. Instead of this it was drawn out to an image five time its breadth. It was moreover no longer white but divided into bands of different colors. He saw immediately that solar light was composite, not simple. He concluded that solar light was a mixture of lights of different colors, of different degrees of refrangibility.

There is no color generated by any natural body whatever. Natural bodies have showered upon them, in the white light of the sun, the sum total of all possible colors and their action is limited to the sifting of that total, the appropriating *form* of the colors which really belong to them, and the rejecting of those which do not. It is the portion of light which they reject, and not that

---

[24] Possible reference from *The Elements of Drawing* published 1856 by John Ruskin

[25] Possible reference to the Greek god Helios.

[26] Norse Mythology, 13th century, Bifrost of Norse Mythology represents a bridge connecting the world of man to that of the gods. It is guarded by the demigod Heimdall.

which belongs to them, that gives bodies their colors. What is the meaning of blackness? It is the result of the absorption of all the constituents of solar light. Pass a red ribbon through a spectrum. In the red light the ribbon is a vivid red, because the light that enters the ribbon is not quenched or absorbed, but in great part sent back to the eye. If that same ribbon is placed in the green of the spectrum, it is black as jet. It absorbs the green light, and leaves the space on which it falls intense darkness. And so it would be with all the colors of the spectrum.

Solar light, reflected from the surface of even a black body is white. The moon appears to us as if,

· "Clothed in white samite, mystic, wonderful,"[27]

"but were she covered with the blackest velvet she would still hang in the heavens as a white, shinning upon our world substantially as she does now."[28]

White light is not simple in its composition, but is the result of a mixture of colors. Newton was the first to recognize the true import of this phenomenon. The colors of which white light is composed may be separated by refraction. The separation is due to the different degree of *deviation* which colors undergo by refraction. Red is the least refrangible color. Then follow orange, yellow, green, blue, and violet in the order of their refrangibility. This separation of white light into its constituents is called dispersion. The number of colors of which white light is composed is really infinite but we have a name for only six of them.

The composition of white light has been ascertained by the process of analysis; it can be verified by synthesis; that is the colors after dispersion may be reunited, and the result of the reunion is white light.

In the case of pigments the light is reflected at the limiting surfaces of the particles, but it is in part absorbed within the particles. The reflection is necessary to send the light back to the eye; the absorption is necessary to give the body its color. The rose is red in virtue, not of the light reflected from its

---

[27] Reference from *Morte d'Arthur* published 1838 by Alfred Lord Tennyson, 1809-1892

[28] Possible reference from *Six Lectures on Light*, lectures delivered in the United States in 1872-1873 by John Tyndall, prominent 19th century physicist

surface, but of light which has entered its substance, which has been reflected from surface within. All bodies, even the most transparent, are more or less absorbent of light. The color of pigments is due to the rays which they absorb least readily. The color of bodies depends generally upon their molecular structure.

The color of light is determined by the corresponding wave-lengths. The light waves diminish in length from the red to the violet. As pitch depends on the frequency with which aerial waves strike the ear, so color depends upon the frequency with which ether- waves strike the eye. The difference between red and violet is a difference analogous to the difference between a high note and a low note on a piano.

How much of the beauty of our world depends upon the sun. To it we owe our light, and were it not for that light where would be the beauty of our flowers, the blue of the sky, the roseate hues of dawn, the saffron and crimson tints which preceed the shadows that steal across the sky and bring the mystic twilight. The sun has well been called "both eye and soul"[29] of this great world.

---

[29] Possible reference from *Six Lectures on Light* by Tyndall

The Building Gifts

The First Gift

Before any course of education can be decided upon, it is necessary to know what the mind requires. To know the needs of the mind particularly the mind of a young child is an important factor, because it is only in this way that a proper development can be attained. Whatever means we use to develop the child's mind should be that which will represent as nearly as possible the outside world, in order that he shall know the relations existing in that world.

The child being a living moving creature we appeal to his activity first of all; then to his reflection in order that the thing which appealed to his activity may take definite hold upon his mind; classification is the next step, for after reflecting upon things he will begin to classify objects; then when sees things in their different classes he will naturally reproduce them; the last two steps in this direction are transformation and definition.

When making up this Gift Froebel worked from two standpoints. The first thing to be considered is what we shall have for an object to teach the child in this Gift. Then what shall it represent to the child from the world. First of all the child's mind must be considered. Moving objects always attract children more than still objects do. The reason of this is because the child is a moving thing himself. The object we want here must be simple and one that can move freely. It should be an object which will represent as many things in the outside world as possible.

The child should be given an idea of certain standard qualities. Form is the general quality by which we know most about a thing. We have found that the curve linear represents the most forms in the world. The simplest form is the sphere and that is the reason why Froebel used the ball.

The balls are made of worsted because that is a material suitable for the small child to handle. Another advantage this material has is that different colors can be used.

In its relation to what follows we must know why the ball is used. The new idea of each Gift is emphasized in the following Gift. There exists in the First Gift implicitly all the ideas that will be brought out in the other Gifts.

In making known this Gift we describe it in two ways. We mean by that that we give it an external and an internal description. The external description could be given by anybody who knew anything about a ball. An internal description could only be given by somebody who knew what the ball represents to the child that is to show its use in regular order of things and its relation to the child's world.

There is contrast in this Gift leading to abstraction. In order to abstract any quality there must be at least one contrast. The quality that we want the child to abstract from the ball is form. The advantage of having all the colors here is to bring before the child the idea that the balls can be all alike in one respect and different in another. Form is the property of matter we would bring before the child here. He can abstract this idea more easily by this contrast of colors, because he sees immediately that the balls are all round but are not all one color.

The salient characteristics of this Gift are unity and moveableness. The ball is alike all over, and it gives us the idea of unity more than anything else.The human mind craves unity. The world should be held up to the child with this idea uppermost, so that he may feel the relation of things in the world.When we come to the cube there is more complexity and for this reason we give the child the simple form of the ball.His mind is not ready yet for anything more complex.

The salient characteristic of this Gift are moveableness and unity. As the object of the Gift is to represent as many things in the world as possible moveableness is an important quality. There are so many moveable things in the world. Everything accomplished in the world is done by moving objects. Even in the mental world there is a circular movement that is the mind goes out as it were and fixes itself upon something.The idea of the object upon which the mind is centered comes to the brain thus making a circular course.

The ball represents another important thing and that is unity. The ball is the simplest means by which this quality is represented. It is alike all over which makes the idea easy for the child to grasp. As it is natural for the human mind to want unity there must be unity throughout the world; therefore the object of this Gift being to represent to the child as much of the world as possible the idea of unity must be held up. The reason that this Gift is presented to the child at this stage is because it is the simplest form and corresponds to the child's mind at this stage. Just at this stage his mind is simple and is not prepared for anything more complex. There is only one thing to be said about the ball, it is round. There is nothing to differentiate. The child's mind at this point is not developed enough for differentiations, so the other Gifts would not be suitable for him now. Froebel considered the ball as the corresponding part to the child's mind in its first stage of development. The undivided unity of the ball corresponds to the child's mental constitution. Its moveableness corresponds to the child's "constructive activity."[30]

---

[30] Possible reference from *Froebel Gifts*

The Second Gift

In the First Gift the main idea is that the child learns there is a difference between himself, the ego and the non-ego.He makes his first distinction.The next step he takes is to distinguish between objects. If this is the next step he must have an object to teach him this. All knowledge comes through differentiation. As we trace differences we trace likenesses as well.In presenting the Second Gift we give the child the sphere, then the cube. The child is familiar with the ball of the First Gift and easily discovers the likeness between ball and the sphere of the Second Gift, but he finds new qualities, hardness resonance. So he finds a connection between the old and the new. Then on account of the great contrast the cube is presented. We give the child broad distinctions, he can not see delicate ones. The cylinder is a crude mediation; it represents equally the two extremes, the sphere and cube.

The Second Gift is related to the First by the sphere. It is the external relationship. The Second Gift is merely carrying on the process of differentiating still farther. With the First Gift the child distinguishes between himself and the objects of the world. In the Second Gift he distinguishes between the objects of the outside world.

All education consists of turning that which is potential into reality. It is possible for a child to practice that law. Froebel works upon the idea that children live up to a law before they are conscious of that law, or understand the philosophy of it. Doing always precedes formulating. Art comes before science.

Sphere has length breadth and thickness but they are all alike. The cube brings out the dimensions more clearly. Everything in nature is on the curve. The reason that Froebel used these three objects is that the sphere can represent God's work, the cube man's work, the cylinder with the roundness of the sphere, the plainness of the cube, the ability to roll and to stand still is the connection between the sphere and the cube. The child has learned that the cube with its many parts is not like his sphere. He has learned the cube in its complexity. Two unconnected opposing ideas have come to the child and to him in his small idea of the world things are disjointed. Then he finds the cylinder which, with its connections between sphere and cube, points him to the connection between his two opposing ideas.His little world is composed of many parts though still a unit. The child has unconsciously found the great law of mediation. He understands nothing of the philosophy of it but like the early race he recognizes the how without understanding it.

It is this great law of mediation that keeps the world in time. The plant sinks its root down into the earth and darkness, it shoots up into the air and light, and both unite in the safe life of the whole plant. The dominant positive do in music and the light far reaching sol are made into a perfect whole by the gentler me which unites them in the chord. All this the child is learning through his sphere, cube and cylinder. These concrete forms are very imperfect representations of these ideas but they serve to start the process of discrimination.Through them the child has the beginning of all knowledge, for "we discriminate only that we may comprehend, we comprehend only that we may build up again."[31] In mental reconstruction the child has found unity in its great variety and that is the end of philosophy. Through these crude representations the child is developing his power of discrimination.

---

[31] Possible reference from *Froebel Gifts*

The Third Gift

The third gift is a two-inch cube divided into eight one inch cubes. The child having had the first and second gifts is how ready for the third. With the first and second he could only represent things. Now he has reached the state where he wants to investigate and construct. The third gift meets this need of the child. It is the first of the building gifts, and meets two strongly marked tendencies of the child; the desire to investigate and to construct. The building gifts are the third, fourth, fifth, and sixth.

The things the child makes with the third gift may often represent but fairly the idea he intends, but he is satisfied because his mind is so simple.

By this two inch cube we give the child an outer and an inner description. He sees the cube as a whole. He knows it is a cube and has sharp edges, faces and corners. The inner description is the illustration of an organic principle.

All plants in the world are divided into two classes, the monocotyledon and *dicotyledon*. By going into the differentiation we narrow the class all the time. A plant is an inanimate, corporeal substance. But when we speak of an animate, organic, corporeal substance connected with the word rational we know immediately it is man.

Another illustration of specialization is geometric figures. Take them in reference to their number of sides, the paralleloism of their sides, the relative size of their angles, the equality of their sides as a basis of differentiation. We speak of the polygon, but it does not call to our mind any particular figure; but when we speak of the quadrilateral and triangle, specializations of the polygon, a four sided and a three sided figure respectively come into our mind. There is still something more to be said about the quadrilateral and the triangle before we can have a definite idea about them.

We have the parallelogram and as soon as we hear the word we know it is a special quadrilateral whose opposite sides are parallel and equal. We can still get more definite information about the quadrilateral. When the parallelogram is right-angled it is called a rectangle. When the four sides of the rectangle are equal it is called a square. When the parallelogram is not right-angled it is called a rhomboid and when the sides of the rhomboid are equal it is called a rhombus.

As we narrow a class down we get more definite information about the thing. The child's knowledge must grow through specialization. In the third gift the child sees before him the cube. He learns that it has six faces, twelve sharp edges, and eight corners. He now knows that these things make the cube. This gives him a lesson in variety and unity. There is unity in the variety of the characteristics, and there is variety in the unity.

The cube in this gift stands for an organic principle. A whole in which the parts are mutually related and vitally dependent upon each other is a definition of an organism. Society is an organism. The child is certainly a member of a society, and is therefore a member of an organism. To do his duty properly in that society he must be taught to see its relationships. Froebel argues that the experiences of life will come easier to the child if he is made acquainted with them through crude illustrations. Through this gift the child receives the value of these illustrations.

The characteristics of the whole cube pervades every one of the eight small cubes. In an organism the life of the whole pervades every part. *Agassiz*[32], the naturalist, says that if he is given any bone of an extinct animal he can tell what it is. Artists can tell a statue of Venus from a Juno simply by an eyebrow, which goes to show how the life of the whole pervades every part. What has this to do with the child? It has everything to do with him, because he is a part of a great whole. It is of the utmost importance that he should be taught that he must do his part properly in that great organism of which he is a part. If he

---

[32] **Jean Louis Rodolphe Agassiz** (May 28, 1807 – December 14, 1873) was a Swiss-born American biologist and geologist who is recognized as a scholar of Earth's natural history.

does not learn this lesson others will suffer as well as he.

In the kindergarten how does the life of the whole pervade every part? In what respect is the definition of an organism applicable to the kindergarten? The kindergarten is an organism and each child is a part of it. Then the parts are mutually related and dependent upon each other. Unless each child acts in harmony with the other children the whole will be affected. He must learn that he is a means as well as an end. He must throw off all idiosyncrasies. The teacher who is successful in bringing this about will not dwell too much on the institutional side, but on the individual as well. There must be an even balance.

We progress from the homogeneous to the heterogeneous. The higher the organism the more heterogeneous it is; the lower the organism the more homogeneous. The higher the organism the more restricted its functions; the lower the organism the more general its functions. Domestic economy is an illustration. The duties of a domestic of a wealthy household are more specialized than those of a servant of a family of limited means.

An organism suggests a type which is never realized. The fruit growing on one tree is all different. There are not two persons in the whole human family alike. In all the different forms of government we never find the ideal. Where there was once absolute monarchy the power has been distributed. Where the father once had the power of life and death over his family, that power no longer belongs to an individual.

An organism develops from the indefinite to the definite, from the simple to the complex, from the homogeneous to the heterogeneous, from unity to variety. This characteristic of an organism is a life principle.

Just as an organism develops the gifts have progressed. Froebel prepares the child by presenting the gifts as a whole. In this gift he shows the cube, and shows that each part is related to every other part.

The child must not be allowed to think that the measurement of every cube is two inches because this cube is two inches.Let him see by contrast in size that all cubes have the same essential characteristics. We teach some lessons better by contrast. With the Third Gift we can teach the child the geometric figures, the cube, prism, and *parallelogram*.

There is a relation between the child's mind and the gift. The mind of the child is an organism and the inner description is an illustration of an organic principle. The mind of the child being an organism it must proceed from the indefinite to the definite, from the simple to the complex, from the homogenous to the heterogeneous, from unity in uniformity to unity in variety. The child's mind has advanced to a higher state now and as he has reached the investigative age very little which is said or done escapes him.

To him the outer explains the inner. We should not say what we do not mean when a child is present. He should not be allowed to see any act of deceit, for to him deceit does not exist.Children and animals are the best of friends because they are closely related in that they show their inner selves by their actions. Children and animals are consistent; man is often not so.

The Fourth Gift

The Fourth Gift is a two inch cube divided by one vertical and three horizontal cuts, producing eight equal parallelepipeds.Each of these parallelepipeds is two inches long, one inch broad, one half inch thick.

Both the third and the fourth gifts are two inch cubes. The third gifts is divided equally once in each dimension, while the fourth gift is divided once vertically and three times horizontally. All the faces of the third gift are divided in four equal squares. Those of the fourth into oblong faces. In the third gift the parts are cubes like the whole. In the fourth the parts are parallelepipeds like each other but unlike the whole. The cubes of the third gift are one inch cubes. The parallelepipeds of the fourth are twice as broad and one half as thick as the cubes of the Third Gift. Both gifts divide naturally into halves, fourths, and eighths, but the fourth gift leads to a clearer grasp of the idea of fractional parts, by the association of each part with a greater variety of forms and positions.

In the third gift the child having been awakened to organic connection will be interested in following the law of organic development. He is not yet prepared for complexity in number, therefore Froebel does not increase the amount of material, but its form; he keeps before the child the idea of unity in the fundamental form and in this way introduces variety in the parts.

In this gift there is a difference in dimension which results in difference in form. The horizontal is distinguished from the vertical. The rectangles is emphasized by difference in dimension. In the Fourth Gift we have the same number as in the third, but in a different form. In the fourth we have the numbers two and its multiples to sixteen.

The mental effect of sequence of symmetry is logical thought. With the third gift the child makes things and can call them almost anything he likes.In the fourth gift there is greater definiteness, which restricts suggestiveness. Through this restriction the child's mental powers are taxed. His imagination, creative powers and observation are trained.

The salient characteristic of the Fourth Gift is difference of dimension in the parts resulting in the abstraction of the idea of length, breadth and thickness.

The forms illustrated in the Fourth Gift are the solid (the cube, square prism, rectangular parallelepiped), the plane (the two rectangles).

In the third gift the faces of the cube are alike and like the whole. In the fourth the faces of the bricks are like each other but unlike the whole. In this there is an organic principle. We have gone from unity in uniformity to unit in variety.

The special point in which this gift is an advance upon the third in its relations to the child is that he has to exercise his mental powers to get every part in its proper relation to the other parts.

The Fifth Gift

The Fifth Gift is a three inch cube divided equally twice in each dimension producing twenty-seven one inch cubes. Three of these cubes are divided into halves by one slanting cut, and three are divided into quarters by two slanting cuts (triangular prisms).

It is an extension of the Third Gift in that it has vertical and horizontal cuts. It differs from the Third in the following points; the Third is a two inch cube, the Fifth is a three inch cube; the Third is divided once in each dimension, the Fifth twice in the Third the parts are like each other and like the whole, in the Fifth the parts differ from each other and from the whole. The Fourth Gift emphasizes vertical and horizontal divisions producing rectangular solids.

The Fifth Gift introduces the diagonal which is the mediations between the vertical and the horizontal. The Fifth Gift by the introduction of slanting lines extends the elements of form. Froebel's idea is to present contrasts to each other but he does not stop there. He gives broad contrasts and then the mediation.

In form the Fifth is related to both the Third and Fourth in being a cub. In number the Third and Fourth both had two and its multiples; the Fifth has three and its multiples. In going to a new idea we ought not to lose sight of the old, so for this reason we have the number two and its multiples in the cubes which are cut in halves and quarters.

The cube divided by the vertical lines of the top face gives us three square prisms. When it is divided by the horizontal cuts it gives us three square prisms, the first consisting of nine whole cubes, the second consisting of six whole cubes, and the three cubes cut in halves by the diagonal cut, the third consists

58

of six whole cubes, and three cubes cut in quarters by the two diagonal cuts.

When the cube is divided into layers the first layer consists of nine whole cubes, the second of nine whole cubes, and the third of three whole cubes and three cut in halves and three cut in quarters.

The Third Gift gave a general impression of vertical and horizontal directions the Fourth gave a contrast between cuts—on vertical and three horizontal. Thus by contrast-differentiating the vertical from the horizontal. The salient characteristic of the Third Gift is, contrast of size; of the Fourth difference of dimension; those of the Fifth are the introduction of the diagonal cut and the division into thirds, ninth, and twenty-sevenths.

We should begin to use this Gift by building forms of life. In this way we are following the history of the race; doing preceeds knowing; construction preceeds analysis, man also does before he formulates.

Corresponding with the child's increasing powers of analysis Froebel offers in the Fifth Gift increasing complexity corresponding with his increasing powers of creation. This Gift offers a higher unity through a greater variety than was illustrated in the previous Gifts.

The Sixth Gift

The Sixth Gift is the last of the building gifts.It consists of a three inch cube composed of twenty-seven rectangular parallelepiped two inches long, one inch wide, and one half inch thick. Of these eighteen are whole parallelepiped, three are divided lengthwise into six half inch square prisms, and six are divided breadthwise into twelve one inch square prisms.

The cubes *are* arranged in three piles of bricks, one of square prisms, and one of square prisms and pillars. The cube is built in such a way that when the box is lifted off, the child sees immediately on the top face three bricks, one square prism, and two pillars. At the first glance he sees exactly what composes the cube.

The Sixth Gift is connected with the Second Gift in form, color and material. It is connected with the Third Gift in being a divided cube, and having the faces of the square prism. The Sixth Gift is an extension of the Fourth Gift from which it differs in the following points. The Fourth Gift is a two inch cube while the Sixth Gift is a three inch cube. The Fourth is divided into undivided parallelepiped; the Sixth is divided into divided and undivided parallelepipeds.In the fourth Gift the parts are similar to each other but unlike the whole. In the Sixth the parts differ from each other and from the whole. In the Fourth Gift are emphasized the number, two and its multiples, while in the Sixth are emphasized two and three and their multiples.

The Sixth Gift is connected with the Fifth Gift in that it is a three inch cube. Both the Fifth and Sixth Gifts have divided and undivided material. In the Sixth the parts are unlike each other and unlike the whole as they are in the Fifth Gift. Both the Fifth and Sixth Gifts have complexity of division. The

Sixth can be divided into thirds just as the Fifth can. The Fifth and Sixth are both adapted to architectural building, the Sixth is especially so. It is not as complex as the Fifth because it has not the slant line.

The pillar or column is the new form introduced in the Sixth Gift. The Third and Fourth Gifts have the number two and its multiples, the Fifth has three and its multiples, while the Sixth has a combination of two and three because the number six is carried all through the gift. Six is the new number in this gift, but it is the multiple of two familiar numbers.

The material of this gift is divided in such a various way that the child's attention should be directed to the proportion of size. We have the brick, the square prism, and the pillar. The square prism is a half of the brick. It takes two square prisms to make a brick, and two pillars will make a brick. The child should compare the forms with each other, first the square prism with the brick, then the pillar with the brick, then the pillar with the square prism. Only the faces of the forms differ in size. The edges differ also.

This gift illustrates the law of mediation of contrast. Here the mediation is in the number six which is composed of two familiar numbers. In this gift there is unification of form as well as number.

The salient characteristics of this gift are, the analysis of the parallelepiped showing the proportion of the different parts in relation to size; the division of the cube into sixths, twelfths, and thirty-sixths; and the forms so well adapted to architectural building. The new form is the pillar.

The idea of form is developed through the fitness of the material for building. In the Third gift the child can do anything within the number eight; in the Fourth anything within sixteen; in the Fifth anything within thirty-nine, while in the Sixth he can do anything within the number sixty.

The Seventh Gift

The Seventh Gift consists of circular, square and triangular planes made of wood. Of the latter there are four varieties, the right isosceles, the equilateral, the right scalene, and the obtuse isosceles.

The circle is the plane of the sphere. The square is the plane of the cube. The right isosceles triangle is one half of the square. It has one 90 degree angle and two 45 degree angles. The equilateral triangle comes from the seed of the cube. It is a plane of the tetrahedron. Each of its angles is 60 degree. The right scalene triangle is derived from the equilateral triangle.It is just half of the equilateral. It has one 60 degree angle, one 30 degree angle, and one 90 degree angle. The obtuse isosceles triangle is one third of the equilateral. We get it by bisecting the angles.

How is this Gift related to the previous gifts? The idea of the solid is given in the previous Gifts and also that of the organic principle. In the Seventh Gift we have unrelated elements. The question as to why Froebel should introduce unrelated elements at this point presents itself. As the idea of the solid has been carried out in the six previous Gifts, the Seventh Gift illustrating unrelated parts of the plan or surface seems to be a contradiction.

The first six Gifts known as the Building Gifts present to the child divided units from the parts of which he constructs new wholes. In this way he becomes familiar with wholes and parts and is prepared for the Seventh Gift. This Gift does not give to the child objects to be transformed. It gives him independent elements to be constructed into various forms. The idea of the relation of the part to the whole already exists in the child's mind, so when he sees unrelated elements in this Gift he recognizes their relation to the whole, so it is plainly seen that Froebel does not contradict himself at this point.

The salient characteristic of this Gift are the presentation of the plane or surface, and color. It is important to cultivate the sense of color, because apart from its artistic value it enters into the occupations of man. The Seventh Gift leads the child from the object to a representation of the object and this prepares the way for drawing.

This Gift is essentially mathematical. The geometric forms illustrated with this Gift are numerous. We have the circle, and we have the square illustrating two rectangles. With the right isosceles triangle we make the rhomboid, the trapezoid, the trapezium, the pentagon, and the hexagon. With the equilateral triangle, the rhombus, the rhomboid, the trapezoid, the pentagon, and the hexagon are illustrated. With the right scalene triangle we make a rectangle, an obtuse isosceles triangle, an equilateral triangle, a rhombus, a rhomboid, a trapezoid, a trapezium, a pentagon, and a hexagon. With the obtuse isosceles triangle the equilateral triangle, the rhombus, the rhomboid, the trapezoid, the trapezium, the pentagon, and the hexagon can be made.

When the Seventh Gift should be introduced is a question. The child up to this time has seen the plane in connection with the solids which he has used. The child cannot get a conception of the third dimension until he has a contrast.He now receives the plane separated from the solid and gradually abstracts the idea of the plane or surface. Contrast in dimension is emphasized in the face of the brick of the Fourth Gift. For this reason, it is best to present the Seventh Gift after the Fourth has been given is Mrs. Wiggin's idea.

The law of the mediation of contrasts is shown by the contrast in this Gift. An illustration of the law of contrasts is given by the idea of the solid in the previous Gifts and the plane of the Seventh.

The amount of material to be given the child in this Gift depends upon what the child wants to make and his idea of combination.

This Gift is helpful to the child in his meaning because he gets an idea of designing with the tablets. This Gift offers to the child the material with which he can express his ideas.

The Tenth Gift Theory

The Tenth Gift consist of whole and half steel rings of different diameters two, one and a half, and one inches respectively.

The Seventh Gift is the plane of the solid. The Tenth Gift is also an outgrowth of the solid and is the periphery of the sphere and the edge of the cylinder. It is also the edge of the circular plane.

The salient characteristic of the gift is that it represents the curved line apart from the solid. Some forms of life can be made with the rings, but owing to the absence of angles the Gift is adapted to the forms of symmetry rather than to forms of life and knowledge. Any forms of nature where the curve predominates can be made best with the rings.

The forms illustrated in this gift are the circle, concentric circles, and the semicircle. The entire geometry of the circle may be illustrated when sticks are used in connection with the rings.

Because of its curved line this gift will suggest the idea of the beautiful to the child more than any other Gift. Hence the gift will appeal to the artistic nature of the child and help to lead his taste to the ideal.

The Eleventh Gift Theory

The Eleventh Gift consists of sticks which are one fifth of an inch thick, and from one to five inches long.

The previous gifts deal with the solid and the plane. Just as the tablet in the Seventh Gift is the plane of the solid, and the ring of the Tenth Gift is the outgrowth of the curved solid and plane so the stick in this gift represents the edge of the solid. Here the child receives the embodied straight line separated from the solid or plane.

The previous gifts have more definite characteristics. By their characteristics they suggest their use where the stick does not.

The salient characteristics of this gift are the representation of the line and the relation of forms and positions. Sometimes the sticks are colored. The advantage of the use of color in this gift is that number can be brought out easily by the contrast of the colors.

With the sticks can be made all the right lined geometric plane figures. This gift is used very early in the kindergarten. It prepares the way for elementary drawing. The strongest feature of this gift is illustrative work. The child can reproduce so many different objects with the sticks. Form and numbers hold subordinate positions in this Gift. It requires great play of the imagination sometimes to grasp the idea which the inventions with the solids intent to give, while the sticks are instantly suggestive in invention.

One way to make the child see the relation of stick to the solid is in *his*-work. The child having worked with the solids after a reasonable time will see from which solids the line is derived.

It requires an amount of manual dexterity to manipulate the sticks, and for this reason care should be taken to avoid tension of muscle and nervousness. By means of this gift the kindergartener can find out the child's impressions of the forms which he has had in the solids.With the stick the child can make all kinds of geometric figures thus reproducing what he has had in the solid and plane. This would serve as a good review for him.

The sticks also offer a good opportunity for calculation. It is readily seen how easy it is for a child to count by means of sticks. It was one of the earliest means of calculation, so in this respect the child is repeating racial history.

The law of the mediation of contrasts is illustrated in this gift. The line is the connection of two opposite points which makes it the mediation.

This gift is good to be used in elementary number work. By practice with the sticks the ideas of form, which the child has received in the other gifts are fixed in his mind. It is also good practice for the elements of designing. It also serves as an introduction for sewing and drawing.

Good lessons in imitation, in dictation, in memory and in invention can be given in this gift. The lessons in imitation test the power of observation. When the child is told to reproduce an object his ability to do the thing will show the extent of his observation. The lessons in dictation can be given in the same manner that the lessons in imitation are given. A memory lesson of course means doing all the work entirely from memory. The children are often told to make anything they please, this is a lesson in invention.

Number, direction, and form can be brought out in all the lessons mentioned alone. Cooperative work is very interesting. The children should work according to the amount of the material they have. The possibilities of a certain number of sticks should be exhausted before that number is increased. Tracing the wood of which the stick is made back to the forest makes a very interesting introductory lesson. Giving the connected facts of the history of the little wooden stick until the tall tree in the forest is a picture in his mind will likely enhance the value of the plain little stick. There is a greater liberty in the gift than there is in any other.

The Child and the Moon

The group of songs known as the light songs are classed together because they all represent truths of spiritual apprehension. In the preceding songs the mother has taken the initiative. In this song she is in the background.

Because the song representing the mother, as responding for the moon teaches her what to do. There is absence of motto in this song because it is evident that all children want the moon. It has such attraction for them that it will divert their attention when they are fretful, and quiet them when restless. In the song the mother responds for the moon. The mother does two things in her conversation, she teaches that everything must do that which is required of it in its own place, and that everybody must "do his duty in that state of life unto which it has pleased God to call him."[33] Here a reciprocal relation is established between the child and the moon. The moon sends its bright greeting to the child, and the child in return must be good and true.

For the child's development it is necessary to enlarge his relations. It is not good for the child that the mother keeps him too closely to herself. If he is kept with her constantly his experiences are limited.

The child has conscious perception of the moon. That brightly shining tall in the sky looks very pretty to him, indeed he thinks he would like to have it. He tries to reach it as though it were a ball within his grasp. The principle illustration we find here is the same as that in The Fisher. The swimming fishes had great attraction for the child. He was not satisfied until he had possession of one. The fish out of the water had lost its charm, because the life

---

[33] Possible reference from the works and sermons of Reverend Thomas Wilson, 1663-1755

67

which was the attraction was gone. This shown that it was not the material thing the child wanted but rather the spiritual possession.

It is the same thing with the moon. It is natural for the child to make the mistake of desiring the external possession, because he must have the thing itself or a conscious perception of the thing before he can have the spiritual possession. The mother excites this desire because while she knows that it can never be gratified in the way the child imagines, still it will lead to the highest conception of spiritual possession. It is for this reason that the other excites in her child a desire for external possession. It will lead him to the high idea of the spiritual.

The lesson this song teaches is obedience to law. As the child calls to the moon to come down to him the moon answers that its place is in the sky and

"If your part you'll do,

I will do mine;

Yours, to be good and true;

Mine, Just to shine!"[34]

This song is intended to show how the moon may be used as a means of developing the spiritual attraction of which it is the "vanishing symbol."[35]

---

[34] *Froebel Gifts*

[35] Ibid

The Boy and the Moon

In the preceding song the mother responded for the moon, while in this one the child responds. The absence of the motto of the preceding song is accounted for in that it needed no interpretation for no mother is ignorant of the attraction of the moon for her child. Where the mother took the initiative in the Child and the Moon, the child takes it in this song.

A child stretches out his hand to grasp the heavenly light. When he does this he has no idea of the distance between him–and the shining object. He is utterly wanting in this respect. Froebel's idea is for the child to get the sense of union before that of distance. A child believes himself to be at one with all things. He is confronted by objects the nature of which he is not able to comprehend but–accepts with simple faith the explanation given by his elders. The wonder created in the soul by the presence of the heavenly lights opens a way by which the child may be given some understanding of their Creator. This lack in the child of appreciating distance is not amiss, but rather by it a higher truth is taught.

The mother may provide a means by which the real relation and distance of this light may be appreciated. She may create in her child sympathetic emotions which will form a ladder upon which he may climb step by step up to the true light of which the moon is only a symbol.

There is a relation in this song to "The Children on the Steeple" which teaches that we do not rush up to heights unknown but go step by step.

It is natural to suppose that Froebel's choice of a boy in this song is because it is more in keeping with real life for a boy to be connected with the idea of climbing.

The child is at an age now when his experience is to be widened. He should be lead to delight in external objects, and also to learn the qualities of those objects. What we want to do is to lead him from the objects themselves to the real life. We have an illustration of this truth in the history of the race. The heathens have worshiped the forces of nature thinking they were the real life.We have a few circumstances sometimes to judge by and from that we form conclusions without knowing anything of the process. The chief lesson intended to be taught by this song is given in the motto.

The moon appears not only to childish years to be "Clothed in white samite, mystic, wonderful"[36] but to refer to years as well, then the child's idea of distance "Which holds him in sweet thrall"[37] could make us realize the importance of the words:

"In years to come no childish dream to be at one with all!"[38]

---

[36] ALFRED LORD TENNYSON (1809-1892), *Morte d'Arthur*, line 31.

[37] *Froebel Gifts*

[38] Ibid

The Little Maiden and the Stars

The motto of this song teaches that children love to view relationships. This desire is strong in the child and we must not disturb it, but rather encourage it. It is well to encourage this desire because we should never break down a belief until the one holding it is in a position to receive the higher idea for which that belief stands. Because the inner life of childhood may be developed by the love for imagining that inanimate objects have human life and human relationships. This tendency of the child is a hint that "it is one spirit which lives in all and works through all."[39] The child feels this loving, creating spirit permeating the universe.

Nature and life around the child are to him as a mirror which reflects that which he feels. As he feels this spirit he must express it. For that reason it is natural for the child to impute personal life to objects which attract him.

An important lesson taught by the light songs is that the heavenly bodies cannot come to the child because they can only do their duty by staying in their proper places. It is another expression of "To thine own self be true and it must follow as the night the day, thou canst not then be false to any man."[40] The moon and stars staying in their proper places teach that we can live the more happily and do our duty more by staying in our proper spheres.

Children in their illusions are *often* nearer the truth than we in our scientific facts, "Heaven lies about us in our infancy."[41] Mother and father stand for the

---

[39] Possible reference from *Froebel Gifts*

[40] Shakespeare, *Hamlet*, Scene III Act I

[41] Attributed to William Wordsworth, 1770-1850

highest spirit of love to the child. In this way we account for his imputing the life of mother and father to objects which attract him. This very thing leads to the idea of the love of God. The child feels that loving Spirit before he knows what it really is. It is this faith which the motto teaches.

Children are not introspective. It is the mother's duty to help them see themselves in nature. Life to the child should be a proclamation of love for if he sees life in this respect he will impute the same spirit to the universe. He will express that which fills his heart.

When the child first looks into his mother's face and sees the love expressed there is the beginning of his knowledge of God.

These objects connected with the light can so easily become the key to spiritual relations. As the child is attracted by the moon and stars so in mature years will his soul be attracted by the spiritual light.

In many respects children's ideas and actions correspond to those of the early race. It is particularly so in this case which is shown by our mythical stories.In those stories people stand for nature. The same idea is in the child's actions when he imputes life to inanimate objects.

The Charcoal Burner

The Charcoal Burner is the first of the trade songs. The trade songs come under the same head as the light songs, the reason of this being that we must have a spiritual apprehension before we can do the practical things.

The motto teaches that there is much to be gotten out of little. Man conquers what cannot conquer itself, and in that which is unassuming there may be beauty. The little things of life are not to be put aside because they seem too trivial for thought and consideration. Little things are the important ones because they are the birth of the greater things. "Smallest seeming causes power may wield"[42] and help us by means of the few little things within our grasp to accomplish much within the boundaries of our own narrow lives.

God in his creation did not finish some things but left them for man to finish and bring to their highest possibilities. Wild flowers are an illustration of this. The flower taken in its wild state and cultivated to its highest possibility shows what was left there for man to finish. Nature cannot always realize her potentialities until man comes in and does it for her.

The most important lesson which Froebel would teach in the trade songs is that children should be taught to respect and reverence people who work with their hands for us. In other words there may be beauty in that which is unassuming.

We go from the light songs to the trade songs. The light songs give us the spiritual understanding, the trade songs the practical idea. It is necessary for us to have the spiritual impression before we can do the practical thing.

---

[42] Possible reference from *Froebel Gifts*

The medium between the world of matter and of thought is the hand. It distinguishes man from the brute and lifts him to his high estate. The highest mark of man's development is his ability to carry out in a practical way the highest ideas that exist in his mind. It shows the divine likeness in him. It is God's thought objectified. Man's work will lead him to clearer ideas and will help him gain an increase of the higher power of truth.

The form in which a universal idea is carried out is not essential. When giving the child games to carry out an idea let them correspond to things in the child's life. Those games which are foreign to the child's life are of little value to him. [margin-Miss Blow shows that this subject admits of discussion and she differs decidedly with Mr. Courthope Bowen in this connection, you should read what she says in Symbolic Education].[43] One great factor which makes civilized life of individuals possible is the co-operation of labor.Co-operative life is an unknown thing in savage life. Another important factor is division of labor. These two things make civilized life possible.

Economy of time and economy of labor and material are the results of division of labor. The division of labor is economy of time and material because one man can put all his energy and skill upon the one thing he has assigned to him. This is an improvement to the whole. By this division of labor the individual has more leisure time provided. If one or a few persons had everything of a certain kind of work to do there would never be time for anything else.

The organic principle is illustrated here by the fact that I am needed by everyone and that I need everyone else. The same principle applies to the social world as well.

Children should be taught the dignity of labor. The man with the rough hands is contributing to the welfare of his brothers. We are valued for what we are, not for what we seem to be.

One point brought out by the burning of charcoal is the importance of fire.

---

[43] Miss Susan E. Blow, 1843-1916, opened one of the first Kindergartens in the U.S. She visited Baltimore in 1902 and gave an address to the Baltimore Kindergarten Association at McCoy Hall at Johns Hopkins University. Bowen, another early educator, author and historian is also noted

Fire is a valuable factor in civilized life. It conquers space by means of trains and boats. Our medium of exchange comes through fire. Fire is also used as a symbol of purification. The *Bible* speaks of it as a purifying process. These are only a few of the many uses of fire.

By the development of the practical arts man has gained more time. This development affects not only the physical life but the spiritual as well, for the practical arts prove the hand to be a witness of God's goodness. The child's gratitude and consideration should be awakened for those who labor for us with their hands. He should be taught that labor directly affects his own welfare. Nearly all the comforts he enjoys have cost somebody a great amount of labor. The child naturally takes all this as a matter of course, but he can be given an idea of the work which other people do for him. By pointing out to him these different points his gratitude can be awakened and also a desire to do as much for other people as he has the power to do at all times.

The Carpenter

The idea which was brought out in the Charcoal Burner is still carried on in this song. Both these songs are intended to teach us to honor those who labor for us with their hands.

This song illustrates the organic principle which is necessary in all things. Each member of a family contributes to the activity and happiness of its life as a whole.In the same way a house as a rule is built in such a way that it will suit all domestic duties. A well planned house influences the comfort and happiness of the family it shelters.

The Creator conceived work in the world which he intended that man should finish. It is a part of man's development that he reason out things. There are some things in nature which do not come to perfection without man's assistance.

The finished house is the external representation of the home. The house is the external sanctity of that which is so precious. It represents an organism. This is shown in the construction; first the timber is changed from one state to another, than there is transformation of the boards. By construction the material is all joined into one thing. Material is the external expression of nature. Material reaches its highest state through thought.

Construction represents not only the preparation and change of material, it only stands for what it should when it fulfills its mission.A shop is a symbol of a thought; it stands for commercialism. Public buildings stand for still other relationships as citizenship etc. All relationships start in the home. Last of all the buildings comes the church as it stands for all our relationship to our Maker.

The deep underlying thought of any of the trade songs is that ministry is the great vocation of life. All life is ruled by love. Love is the motive power underlying the world. In this we are imitating our creator. His ruling of the universe is His love for us. "Love is the aim of every human soul."[44] Love manifests itself in service. Children should be taught that they can be grateful to those who do so many good things for them. It is for his good that the carpenter labors. The child realizes that it is pleasant to have a pretty cozy home and how could he have this pleasure without the work of the carpenter. The trade of the carpenter has been honored by the fact that Christ was a carpenter's son.

Froebel probably chose the carpenter as a representative of civil society as buildings are symbols of relationships in life.

The lesson taught by the trade songs is an important one. It is the lesson that respect and gratitude are due to those who labor for us.

"To conquer an unshaking faith in love is the moving principle of the universe as to win the victory of life."[45]

---

[44] Possible reference from Froebel Gifts

[45] Ibid

The Two Gates and the Little Gardener

The Two Gates and The Little Gardener have a common characteristic—thus connection with nature. Each of these little games embodies an important thought. The Farmyard Gate teaches that the child should be taught to prize and protect what he already has by preventing powers from running away with themselves. The motto of the song also teaches that the mother's words and actions have an educational influence upon her child. A child does not always understand the words that are spoken to him but very often they are planted more deeply in his mind than we know for after a while the seeds spring up. The Garden Gate teaches to keep what we have by keeping out all deleterious influences. "The Garden Gate" teaches the value of the child's recognizing and naming the different objects around him. The Little Gardener teaches the value of giving a child something the life of which depends upon his sole care.

The first of these three songs treats of animals; and their actions, the second song treats of flowers and their qualities; and the third song goes back of the actions of the animals and the qualities of the flower to the unseen things, life which makes these phenomena possible.

The relation of man to nature is his mastering of it. Nature is gradually developed by man and in this way he becomes the master. Electricity is an illustration of man's mastery. It is a natural phenomenon but it could not accomplish what it does until man applied its force to his needs. Cultivation of flowers is another illustration. Man learns through comprehension and comprehension comes through use.

The child in order to become acquainted with nature must be brought in direct contact with her. Children's attention must be directed to the characteristics, activities, states and conditions of things. Children will interpret an animal or a thing by the noise it makes. It is well for them to learn that external actions are not always the interpretation.

The first of these songs treats of the actions of animals. The second one is an advance in that it is a development by going from the actions to the qualities. Of these songs Froebel chose the gates as a symbolism of guarding what is already within, and keeping out that which is harmful. The symbolism of the gates is to guard by arming.

At a certain stage of development a child will find or invent names for objects and qualities. This hint given by the child should be obeyed. This tendency to notice objects and their attributes should be encouraged, for powers of the mind not exercised are wasted. A child quickly finds names for things he perceives.

The Little Gardener is an advance over the two gates because it goes farther than actions and qualities and approaches the universal life. Children love gardening. It is their love of caring for things. In this song Froebel would teach us the importance of rendering children "capable of giving nurture."[46] The habit of caring for any particular thing (a plant or an animal) is a great benefit to a child.

"The joy of nurture he will learn,"[47] for if his care has been what it should be, he will be rewarded by the results. He will also get in the habit of doing his best and habit is the best barrier one can have. Plants and animals are good things for which the child should begin to care. "Reason sleeps in plants, dreams in animals, and awakens in man."[48]

---

[46] *Froebel Gifts*

[47] Ibid

[48] Possible Froebelian reference to ancient Hindu proverb "God sleeps in stone, breathes in plants, dreams in animals and awakens in man"

The Knights and the Cross Child

The Knight songs illustrate the breaking up of the physical union for that of something higher between mother and child. The positive side is given by the Knights and the Good Child. The idea of using the knights in expressing the negative side is to emphasize the qualities of the good child. The qualities of both the good and the bad child are clearer when brought out under the same conditions. [margin– I think the same symbolism, viz. the Knights, is used in both songs because the child must realize that all our actions, good and bad, are judged by the same standards; otherwise, if more than one standard were used, the child would become confused].

The object of the Mutter Und Koselieder is to help the child to know and realize his essential self, that is bringing him to what he really should be. The question arises as to how we can know our essential selves. We can only know the essential self as we know everything else. We know things by the universal idea of them. To get this idea we must distinguish the thing from ourselves and look at it from an objective standpoint. The only way the child can get the universal idea of knowing what he really should be is by knowing what other people think. The mother cannot always form a just opinion on this subject because she is hedged in by the love for her child and the narrowness, *this subjects her to give a prejudiced opinion.*

There is a difference between the real child and the essential self. The real child is what he is and the essential self is what he must make himself. The child should know that there is a standard for him to reach. His ability to reach the standard required of him should be made clear. Danger lies in this fact for merit is too often confused with praise. Don't let him believe that a possible achievement already exists when it does not. Here a touch of other lives will help and uplift his own life. The test by which we prove things and actions to be self-sustained is by the judgment of the world at large not simply that of today but by that which has always made known its approval. We cannot always name the thing which is right in ourselves, it must often be named from afar.

The mother's attitude to the child should be such that he will realize that her approval is given to his true self, the actions which express his true nature. The child should see that he is loved not only for what he is but for what he will grow to be as well. A child is incited to do his best by seeing the respect and consideration shown to the good in others. There should be a distinction between a child's actions and their inner motives for he may get a false idea of himself.

The motto-teaches the negative side. If we put ourselves out of harmony with things we are lonely and isolated, cut off from the fellowship of others. We were not created for isolation. Crossness in children often comes from overwrought nerves.

If such is the case, the child is really suffering and he needs the help of a tender care. The best way to help him is to attract his attention quickly. The means used to divert him should be something—not some great noise for that will only irritate his nervousness and excitement—soothing.

The knights are used here because they stand for something strong to the child. The childhood and the knight stands out as a representation of freedom, self-determination, the control of intellectual force, over that of brute force, the horse and beauty. Such being the case the child will strive to be the thing he commends. The commentary teaches that external facts may be the same and affect people in entirely different ways.

Froebel has the same form of judgment in this song and the preceding one in order that the child may see the judgment from the same source.

The Knights and the Mother

The object of the whole system of the Mutter Und Koseleider is to lead the child to perfect self-consciousness. This song like the two preceding ones relates to the bond of union between the child and other people. This song however goes even more deeply into the child's inner life as its object is to make him conscious of the peculiar tie existing between him and his mother. The object of Froebel's continuing the play of the knights in this song is to acquaint the child with the tie between him and his mother through the same symbol which made him conscious of the union between himself and other people in general.If this union between mother and child is not made clear to the child it may deteriorate into merely a physical bond which would be injurious from all points of view.

To know a thing we must see it and objectify. To really see a thing we must put our whole attention upon it. Now if the child puts his whole mind upon the song he will readily recognize himself in it.In the preceding song we learn that it is necessary for the child to know himself. This essential self is not what he is but what he will grow to be. An ideal should be held up to the child and he should be encouraged to believe that he will reach that standard by doing what he should do. He should learn to discriminate between himself an another-and ideal self.

This song teaches the spiritual bond between the child and his mother. It also teaches the bond of union between the child and the universe. The foundation of this bond existing between the mother and child, and between the child and the world is the goodness of a true, strong character. Mother and child are all and all to each other under all conditions, but the power which influences the union between a person and others in general is the strength of character.

In this game the knights want the child to go with them because he is good. The knights do not want to take him riding simply because he is a little boy, but because he is a good child. Goodness makes itself felt. The mother should make the child feel that it is not only because he is her child that she wants to keep him and not let the knights have him. She should teach him that it is his goodness she loves. This will teach him to appreciate the fact that everybody loves a good, true character. In this game the knights represent to the child the value the world puts upon goodness, the mother appreciates in him the same thing. From this he will learn to value the same qualities.

Hide and Seek Song

The fact that Hide and Seek has an inexhaustible charm for children is well known by everybody. The Universalities of hiding games proves that they are deeply rooted in human nature. This shows that they must be of some value in the development of childhood. The root of the pleasure of hiding games is twofold. The child enjoys not only the pleasure of being found, but he feels that he is something apart from the people and things around him. When he hides he knows that it is he who must be found. This song is a continuation of the distinct personality illustrated in the Falling game.

In this hiding game the hiding is a means to an end. This game begets frankness. The child wants to be found and it is this point in the game that should be emphasized. Emphasizing the finding will bring out the frankness of the child's nature. The child must not get the idea that the hiding is the purpose of the game for that is a dangerous point. From this he might get the idea of hiding his thoughts and actions and that is a thing to be guarded against. We should be careful that the child does not find so much pleasure in concealment that he becomes indifferent to being found. This might possibly be the beginning of his wanting to conceal what he knows his mother would not approve but rather condemn.

The source of the pleasure of this game lies in the anticipation of the discovery of the hiding place. The question arises why does the child want to conceal himself from his mother. It surely is not because he wants to be separated from her. Froebel teaches that the child's love for hiding comes from the fact that spiritual union is strengthened by physical separation. The child delights in finding his mother again and expresses great joy when his mother finds him again. It is well to encourage his desire to be found, and to heighten his joy in the reunion.

The universality of the hiding games proves their value. That which will stand the test of time proves its validity. It must be of some use. A baby's food, milk, is an illustration of this. All young children like it and that very idea proves that it is the food for their use. It is the same way with their pleasure. When all children in all ages like to play certain games there is surely something in those games to satisfy something in their development. Only that which calls upon the child for activity is of any use in the kindergarten.

There is such a thing possible as the union between mother and child becoming inordinate and injurious. The child may learn to depend constantly upon his mother and by so doing have a dependent nature. A mother through a selfish love for her child might keep him too closely to her and cause him to have limited experiences.

When we consider the danger of estrangement we wonder why the mother obeys this instinct of hiding her child without the least hesitation. It is simply the mother's way of increasing the spiritual union through physical separation. When the child hides himself he realizes that he is a distinct personality; he is something apart from his mother and his surroundings. This is the beginning of his independence. It is one way of strengthening the spiritual union between mother and child.

The greater the independence of two people, the greater is the bond of union between them.Independence comes through strength of character and the richer the nature by independence, the more there is to love in the person. Giving and taking constitute a complete process. The mother delights in giving her child pleasure by feigning to look for him, but her delight is not full until the child expresses his joy in being found by her. As the child grows more independent the physical union decreases and the spiritual union increases. When the boy becomes a man and fulfills the mother's expectations, then her joy is complete.

Froebel emphasizes the danger there may be in this game and urges us to guard against the child's pleasure of concealment being greater than his pleasure in being found. When the child's hiding place is discovered he realizes that it is he who is being found. He knows that the mother's delight is all expressed for him. The mother should lead her child to make the ego merit its recognition.

The Church and The Little Artist

The motto of this song teaches three things. First it shows how a child will naturally turn to harmony. It points to the fact that parents should nourish this natural impulse. Then it teaches that common striving unites all things. Harmony and happiness are really the same thing. There is so often misapprehension as to the source of happiness. There is a mistaken idea that it must come from our worldly possessions and our surroundings. Happiness depends upon neither of these. "The mind is in its own place and in itself can make a heaven of hell."[49] Happiness comes from our acting in unity with a common law. Out of this very fact grows the definition of happiness; it is harmony with universal life.It is the activity or the work which places us in harmony with life. If we do not act in unity with a common law we are not in harmony with the universal life and unhappiness must follow.

Harmony acts as a magnet in a child. He will shun discord and, as is illustrated in this song, "loves to stay where all things are at one."[50]

In families where church going has any real relation to the home life the children are anxious to go to church. They enjoy the privilege not because they understand what is being said but from the fact that everybody is worshipping in the same manner. The child knows that a common thought is stirring many minds. Here he begins to recognize unity and harmony of life. This is the way we account for the child liking to go to church. The church is a manifestation of God and His universality. The church as all other symbols should be attractive

---

[49] Reference from *Paradise Lost* published 1668 by John Milton, 1608-1674

[50] Possible reference from *Froebel Gifts*

to children.

It is a natural tendency of mankind to acknowledge a common bond. In each life there is or should be, one high endeavor, one consecrated aim.

All children take great pleasure in any assembly of their elders. It is for the simple reason that they feel that they are a part of society or of the life around them. We must bring home to the little ones their relationship to God. This can be done by satisfying and strengthening the prophesies of the soul. Then the child will find:

"The life of all life

The light of all light,

The love of all love.

The good of all good—God."[51]

After setting forth the high and noble thought that each life has one consecrated aim that reshapes each lesser thought, Froebel closes the Mutter Und Koseleider with The Little Artist. In all its forms drawing is pleasing to children. Drawing shows the mind's creative power and offers a simple form for its development. The child has a little world of his own and he must express in some simple way his ideas. By drawing the child goes from perception to picture.In this way he is passing in review before his mind what he has learned in his little life.

There are two things necessary to every life and that is first to discriminate the permanent and essential points in life from the accidental and vanishing elements and by so doing learn to choose what is good and avoid what is evil.

For one to know God he must exercise his own creative power. Drawing will help him to do this because it creates activity. It is necessary to exercise the creative power consciously in order to produce the good. Froebel says doing what is good is the tie between Creator and creature and it is the union of all humanity with God. A complete and true union with God is the beginning and end of all education.

---

[51] ibid

APPENDIX

Appendix 1

Grave marker and obituary from **The Daily Times** *(Salisbury, Maryland) 1975*

Miss Mary Elizabeth (Betty) Humphreys, whose 94th birthday was Thursday, died today in the Wicomico Nursing Home after a long illness. Her home was at 115 Broad St.

Born in Salisbury, she was a daughter of the late Dr. Eugene and Josephine Tarr Humphreys. She was a member of St. Peter's Episcopal Church and for many years had been active in the Red Cross.

There are no immediate survivors.

Funeral services will be held Monday at 11 a.m. in St. Peter's Church with the Rev. Harry Riddle Johnson officiating. Interment will be in Parsons Cemetery.

Arrangements are being handled by the Hill-Baker-Bounds Funeral Home.

Appendix 2

UNITED STATES BUREAU OF EDUCATIO.

BULLETIN, 1914, NO. 2 - - - - - - - WHOLE NUMBER 573

COMPULSORY SCHOOL ATTENDANCE

KINDERGARTENS NOT REPORTED. 87

List of kindergartens for which no statistical data are available.—Continued.

States and cities.	Name of kindergarten.	States and cities.	Name of kindergarten.
Maryland:		Missouri—Contd.	
Baltimore	Egenton Home.	Kansas City	Miss Francis Scott's Kindergarten.
Do	Hampden Free Kindergarten.		
Do	Home of the Friendless.	St. Louis	German Protestant Orphans' Home.
Do	Light Street Free Kindergarten, Nursery, and Child's Hospital.	Do	Girls' Industrial Home.
		Do	Mission Free School, Church of the Messiah.
Cambridge	Mrs. Handby's Kindergarten.	Warrenton	Central Wesleyan Orphan Asylum.
Salisbury	Miss Elizabeth Humphrey's Kindergarten.		
Massachusetts:		Montana:	

Cover and article from the Washington Government Printing Office 1914.

94

Appendix 3

Article from **The Kindergarten News** (*Springfield, Mass*) *1896.*

97

Appendix 4

THE

JOHNS HOPKINS

UNIVERSITY CIRCULARS

1900—1903

———

BALTIMORE
The Johns Hopkins Press
1903

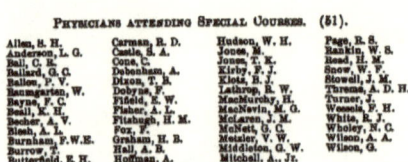

Article from **The JHU Circulars** *which mentions Miss Susan E. Blow*

Kindergarten lecture in Baltimore 1902.

Appendix 5

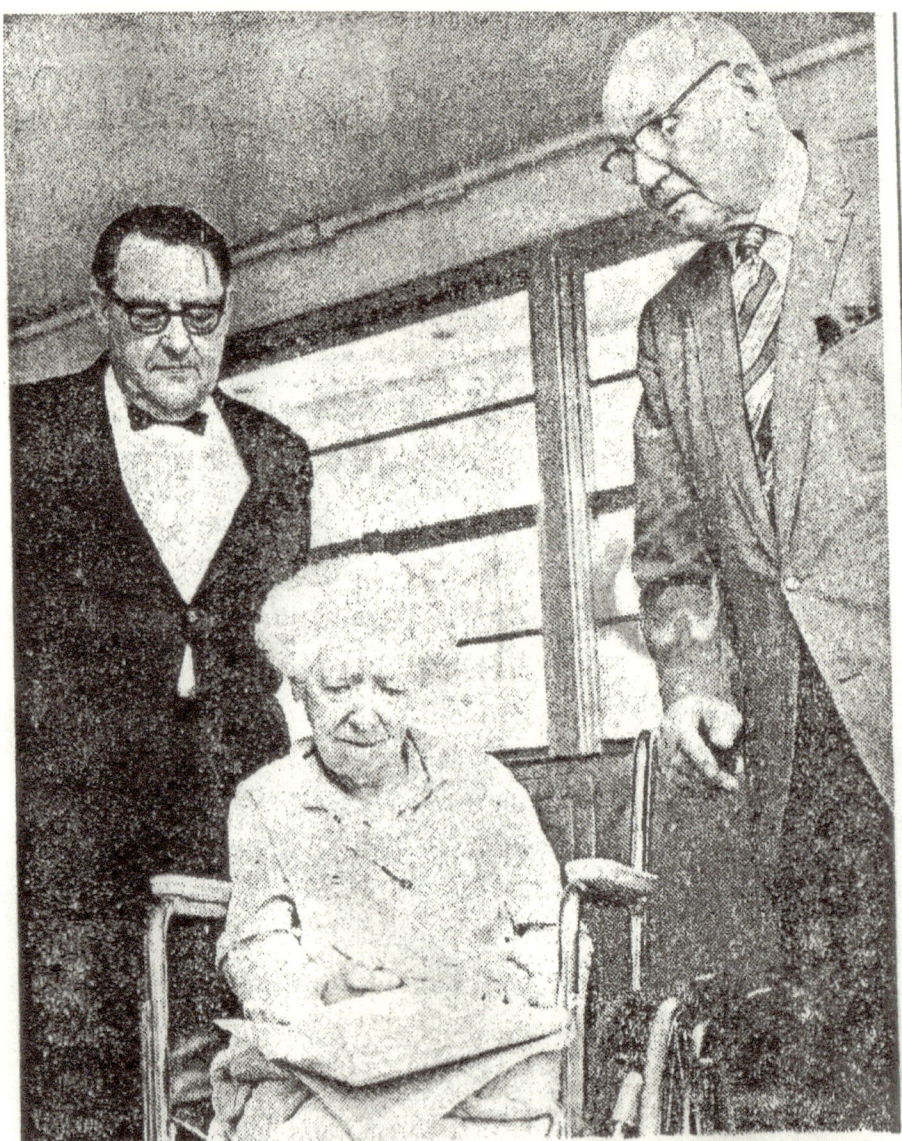

GIFT TO HISTORICAL SOCIETY. Miss Mary Elizabeth (Betty) Humphreys signs letter of gift for an old cannon of Revolutionary War design to the Wicomico Historical Society, John E. Jacob, president, stands on the left, and Rollie W. Hastings, a personal friend, is on the right. The Society will restore the cannon.

Article and photograph from **The Times** *(Salisbury, Maryland) 1973*

APPENDIX 5

Appendix 6

Second Series of Mother Plays

The Target song begins the second series of the Mother Play songs. The Children on the Floor ends this series. The prominent feature of all the preceding songs has been the exhibition of force. Another important feature of the first series is that of relationships. The elementary experiences of the preceding songs are time, space and movement.

In the preceding songs the child advances from unconsciousness to consciousness. He looked at the life of his little world as a matter of fact. When he gradually became conscious of things around him he classified only by means of number, form, and size.

With the Target begins a consciousness of an external world. The child begins to classify in this outside diversity. Here the Target begins an advance. Now definite thoughts are coming to the child. He has advanced from the baby age to the kinder garten age.

The underlying idea of all the songs of the second series is proportion. Proportion is number implied in space. As virtue is to character so is proportion to space. When we speak of virtue we mean all the qualities in a proper proportion. It is really proportionate activity - that is well

Copy of Original Second Series Mother Plays *commentary by Elizabeth Humphreys which now resides in the Nabb Research Center.*

About the Author

Dameon Gibbs holds an BA in Anthropology and World History and an MA in Classical Studies. For the past five years he has worked with inner-city youth in Baltimore, Maryland. He has been an avid writer since his days in high school during the late 1990's. He enjoys the creative process of all writing genres, whether it be religious, poetic, science fiction, historical, biographies or action adventure.

Dameon is married to fellow author Tiffany Michele.

You can connect with me on:

🌐 https://gibbspublishingconglomerate.com

📘 https://www.facebook.com/GibbsPublishing

Also by Dameon Gibbs

As an author, I love to create a variety of worlds in which readers are able to get lost in. From non-fiction, post-apocalyptic earth to the furthermost galaxies, with tales of adventure and discovery in ways we as people can relate to.

Preston Lee Morris: A Soldier, A Man, A Father
Here are written the memories of Preston Lee Morris, spoken himself on the day of September 6, 2014. Mr. Morris intended to pass on his knowledge to later generations. May his words help you look back in America's history, when life was truly different, and then reflect on how you can make the country that much better for tomorrow based on how you live today.

The Bible: Revised King James Version
The Revised King James Version study Bible contains the written notes and thoughts of Donald Peart, a pastor, author and servant of the kingdom. For those that desire the deeper knowledge of the Father, they must read the scripture as it was originally written; which is the purpose of this Revised King James Version.

Found in the Storm

Found in the Storm by Tiffany and Dameon Gibbs is a gripping fictional narrative that seamlessly weaves together themes of betrayal, forgiveness, redemption, survival, and the testing of one's faith. The authors skillfully crafted an exciting and powerful story that keeps readers on the edge of their seats from start to finish.

The protagonist, Antonio, is a character whose perilous journey forms the backbone of the story. He is a very complex individual with strengths and flaws. His decision to join the Army with the hope of improving his life, only to face a dishonorable discharge, sets the stage for a series of challenges that test his resilience and determination. The story cleverly explores the complexities of Antonio's life as he navigates the aftermath of his choices.

The plot takes a turn when Antonio accepts an under-the-table job flying a helicopter, reminiscent of his military days. The seemingly straightforward task of transporting a package from point A to point B in rural Minnesota becomes a high-stakes adventure, especially when a deadly winter storm sweeps in. The authors create a palpable sense of tension and suspense as Antonio grapples with the decision to risk his life for what initially appeared to be easy money. Will he be able to successfully navigate the helicopter through the blinding, severe snowstorm? How will he survive being on the brink of death?

Tiffany and Dameon Gibbs have created an intriguing tale that is both thrilling and thought provoking, with realistic and multifaceted characters that make them relatable and realistic. This story is not merely a tale of survival; it is a profound exploration of human resilience and the pursuit of redemption.

Found in the Storm is a must-read for those who enjoy traversing the twists and turns of a story with a compelling blend of adventure and suspense. This novel will leave a lasting impact, inviting readers to reflect on the intricate tapestry of life and the choices that shape our destinies.

www.ingramcontent.com/pod-product-compliance
Lightning Source LLC
Chambersburg PA
CBHW020319130626
46549CB00003B/927